Jesus' Ministry of Liberation

A Companion after the Year of Mercy

Rev. Fr. Aaron Agbeshie Agorsor

En Route Books and Media, LLC
St. Louis, MO

Visit https://fatheraaron.org today!

ENROUTE
Make the time

En Route Books and Media, LLC
5705 Rhodes Avenue
St. Louis, MO 63109

Cover credit: TJ Burdick

Library of Congress Control Number: 2020936376

Scriptural citations are drawn from the *New American Bible,* St. Benedict Press, Catholic Edition, 1991.

ISBN-13: 978-1-952464-04-1

Nihil Obstat: +John Bonaventure Kwofie Archbishop,
Archdiocese of Accra, Archbishop's Office, P. O. Box GP 247
Adabraka, Accra, Ghana
Cell: +233.20.8137603, Telephone: (030)22.22.

TABLE OF CONTENTS

Reviews i
Dedication iii
Acknowledgments v
Foreword vii
Introduction 1
Chapter One: Ministry is Mercy 9
Chapter Two: Should Not You Have Had Mercy On Your Fellow Servant As I Had Mercy On You 31
Chapter Three: A Priest to Turn to: Blind Bartimaeus' Encounter with Jesus 45
Chapter Four: The Name of God is Mercy 55
Chapter Five: Jesus Comes For Us When We Recognize That We are Sinners 67
Chapter Six: The Quality of Mercy 77
Chapter Seven: Lightening the Load 91
Chapter Eight: Mary, Mother of Mercy 103
Chapter Nine: Mercy in the Light of *Misericordiae Vultus* 115
Chapter Ten: Some Personal Experiences of the Mercy of God 129
Conclusion 145
Appendix: *Misericordiae Vultus* 157
Glossary 187
Bibliography 189
About the Author 191

REVIEWS

"Fr. Aaron Agorsor has a tremendous and practical way of unpacking the Gospel and growing the spiritual life. His lively writing [and speaking] style is particularly effective with new Christians. This book is a must read." — **Very Rev. Fr. Rob Clements, Director, All Saints Catholic NEWMAN Centre, Arizona State University, Tempe, Arizona**

"Please don't simply read this book but breathe it in deeply, absorb it, and put it into action! Ours is a world that seems to be increasingly divided, contentious, leery of "the other," and more often than not filled with fear and discouragement. Is there any reason for hope? Fr. Agorsor reminds us that the Gospel offers to this question a resounding, "Yes!" Hope is found in the faithful, extraordinary love and mercy of the God who not only made all that is, but who out of His unfathomable love became flesh to rescue His creation from the powers of sin, division and death. In these rich reflections, Fr. Agorsor pleads with those who have been rescued to go and rescue others with the same love and mercy that we have so graciously received from God." — **Fr. John Riccardo, Executive Director, ACTS XXIX, www.actsxxix.org**

"What is mercy? For many contemporary Christians, mercy is a very thin concept, connected perhaps to ideas of God lowering his standards or indulging our selfishness. But as Fr. Agorsor shows in this book, Biblical mercy is an endlessly rich concept and reality: in a sense, it is the very Gospel itself. Quoting generously from the Word of God, the successors of Peter, and contemporary Christian writers, Fr. Agorsor explores all the dimensions of divine mercy from the theoretical to the practical, showing how the practice of mercy can be life-transforming for the disciple of Christ. A rich treatment of an unfathomable topic!" – **Dr. John Bergsma, Professor of Theology at Franciscan University, in Steubenville, Ohio**

DEDICATION

This book is dedicated to my parents:
Mr. Brummel Hugh Yaovi Agorsor and Rebecca Abotsi for instilling in me the love of God.

ACKNOWLEDGMENTS

I wish to express my sincerest gratitude to God for his tremendous mercy which endures forever.

I am eternally grateful to Most Rev. Thomas Olmsted, Bishop of the Diocese of Phoenix, for welcoming me into his diocese and giving me the opportunity to exercise my priestly ministry at All Saints Catholic Newman Center.

Gratitude goes to Most Rev. John Bonaventure Kwofie, the Metropolitan Archbishop of Accra, my home diocese, for giving me the Nihil Obstat to this book after painstakingly reading through my manuscript after a short notice.

I cannot forget the invaluable support of Very Rev. Fr. Rob Clements, the Director of the All Saints Catholic Newman Center, for welcoming me to the Newman Center and to his home, God bless you.

Thank you again, Rev. Fr. Dr. Michael Kodzo Mensah, for writing the foreword to this second book and for your invaluable support over the years.

My eternal gratitude goes to Rev. Fr. John Riccardo, Dr. John Bergsma, and Very Rev. Fr. Rob Clements for writing the review to this book.

Appreciation to all who edited the manuscript: Fathers Agbenosi, Pallu, Bulloro, Carbonu, Salifu, Melvin Mensah, Senanu, Raymond Tuvi, Edem Gavor, and Prof. Ayanna Thompson. Thank you, Antionette Neequaye, for typing the manuscript in its initial stages. Gratitude goes to Fathers Destiny Amenuvor, James Ahenkorah, Andrew Obeng, SVD,

Emmanuel Salifu, Julie Carrick, and Raymond Tuvi for sharing your invaluable experience of God's mercy.

I cannot thank you enough, my benefactors, the Hoyt, the Looker, the Lebeau, Wayne, Menefee, Ann, Helena, and Dina families, for providing social, financial, and emotional support for me when I needed it most.

My appreciation goes to Rev. Fathers Kulah, Vinatius, and Alphonsus for providing me with priestly fraternity and community here in Phoenix. For all my friends and family, especially my siblings: Yayra, Vivian, Thomas and his wife Afi, and Nancy, for being such a blessing in my priestly and academic journeys.

My gratitude goes to all the Catholic students and parishioners at the All Saints Catholic Newman Center at the Arizona State University. Our frequent encounters at the confessional motivated the completion of this book.

Finally, I wish to thank Sheila Luna and Professors Ronald Broglio and Lois Brown for providing the needed support in my quest for knowledge.

FOREWORD

For many a Catholic, the very mention of the word "Mercy" immediately evokes the Extraordinary Jubilee of Mercy, which Pope Francis declared on 8th December, 2015, marking the 50th anniversary of the closing of the Second Vatican council. Fr. Aaron Agorsor's book on Mercy, five years after this significant event, is perhaps an important reminder that this theme is evergreen and constantly relevant to our lives as Christians. I herewith congratulate him for the gift of this book to the Church.

The reflections in this book appear to arise from five sources. Firstly, Fr. Aaron leads the reader to reflect on the theme of Mercy arising from the Sacred Scriptures. God reveals himself as merciful (Ex 34:6-7) in the Pentateuch and in the Prophetic Literature he continues to show himself as forgiving, not desiring the death of the wicked but their conversion (Ezekiel 33:11). In the Psalms, the biblical author is conscious of this Merciful God and constantly prays for mercy (Ps 130). The author further demonstrates the face of the Merciful Father in the New Testament with several references to texts such as the Prodigal Son, the Blind Bartimaeus, the conversion of Zacchaeus among others. Indeed, Fr. Agorsor devotes a chapter to the Blessed Virgin Mary chronicling her experience of Mercy from the Magnificat to the foot of the Cross.

Secondly, the author brings on board the experiences of the Fathers of the Church on the question of Mercy. The book contains several references to St. Augustine who taught that "a saint is not a sinless person but a sinful person in search of mercy." The "Confessions" become an important point of reference as Fr Agorsor leads the reader to explore the reality of a life lived in sin vis-à-vis the joy of forgiveness and reconciliation with the Father.

Thirdly, Fr. Agorsor brings us once again to contemplate the writings of ecclesiastical authorities, most prominently Pope Francis. Devoting an entire chapter to Pope Francis' *Misericordiae Vultus*, the author revisits the main themes for the Extraordinary Year of Mercy. Pope Francis invites the church to be Merciful like the Father (Luke 6:36). This mercy of the Father is to be celebrated in the liturgy as instituted by Pope John Paul II on Divine Mercy Sunday; it is to be lived as a value in Marriage, as recommended in the document *Familiaris Consortio*; and it is to be lived out in the workplace as recommended by the document *Laborem Exercens*.

Fourthly, Fr. Agorsor draws on the experiences of a number of modern writers. The range of writers he draws on enriches the work with several perspectives on the question of mercy. Bishops, priests and Lay people are all given a voice especially in the tenth chapter where the author collects personal experiences of colleagues and friends who open up on the question of Mercy. This dialectical approach draws in the reader and prepares us to reflect on our own personal experience of God's Mercy. Mercy is something everyone has experienced and our collective experiences must be shared in order to enhance and deepen our appreciation of this sublime virtue.

Finally, Fr. Agorsor brings his personal touch to this book. In his conclusion, the author lets us in on his motivation for writing the book. He states, "We, priests need mercy, too, as anybody else and the only way to give this mercy out is to open up to experience this mercy ourselves and confidently and faithfully spread this message with joy, hope and authenticity." It is this first-hand experience of God's Mercy and the experience of being its ambassador which has inspired the writer to write this work. Like many a priest, Fr. Agorsor stands in a privileged position to speak on mercy. He has experienced mercy, and he has devoted his life to the mission of helping others to experience same.

Rev. Fr. (Dr.) Michael K. Mensah
Dean of Academics
St. Paul's Catholic Seminary
Sowutuom, Accra.
(Author of *Breaking the Word*)

INTRODUCTION

In his book *Divine Mercy: A Guide from Genesis to Benedict XVI,* Robert Stackpole, PhD, STD, says that the word 'Mercy' in contemporary English has a very restricted meaning. It is usually used to refer to an act of pardon. In the Catholic theology, however, mercy means more than pardon or the cancellation of punishment. Mercy is God's love reaching down to meet the needs and overcome the miseries of His creatures. In the Old Testament, there are two principal Hebrew words that we usually translate as mercy. First of all, there is the word *hesed ((***Hebrew: חֶסֶד**) which means "steadfast love, covenant love." Someone who has the attribute of *hesed* is someone you can always count on; someone who will never let you down. When in the Old Testament the word *hesed* is used of the Lord, this always occurs in connection with the covenant that God established with Israel. "This covenant was, on God's part, a gift and a grace for Israel ... God had made a commitment to respect it ... [this divine *hesed*] showed itself as what it was at the beginning, that is, as a love that gives, love more powerful than betrayal, grace stronger than sin" (no.52). The second most common word for God's mercy in the Old Testament is the Hebrew word *rachamim:* which means tender, compassionate love, a love that springs from pity. Someone who has *rachamim* is someone who feels for your plight and is moved with compassion to help you. *Rachamim* is often used in conjunction with *Hesed.* It comes from a root word *Rechem,* which means a mother's womb. Thus, there is a special intimacy and responsiveness about this kind of love, and a special concern for the sufferings of others. And so when these Hebrew words *Hesed* and *Rachamim* are applied to God, we mean He is steadfast, dependable, righteous, true to Himself and to his promises. He is tender responsive and compassionate like a mother responding in love to the sufferings of her children. In Akan, we call it "Abadaye;" the Ewe call it "Dometrotro." In the New Testament, the Greek word that is usually translated as "mercy" is the word *Eleos*. It can also be translated as loving kindness or tender compassion. The Greek word comes from a root word meaning oil that is poured out. Thus, when the Church sings in her liturgy the Greek words 'Kyrie Eleison' and 'Christie Eleison,' she is praying that the merciful love of God will be poured out upon her children, like holy oil from above. Father Cantalamessa Preaching the 4th Lenten Sermon of the Papal Household in 2007 has this to say of mercy:

> For a community, forgiveness is what oil is for a motor. If one drives a car without a drop of oil, after a few kilometers everything will go up in flames. Forgiveness that lets others go is like oil. There is a psalm that sings of the joy of living together as reconciled brothers; it says that this "is like perfumed oil on the head" that runs down into Aaron's beard and clothing to the very hem (cf. Psalm 133).

The fathers of the Church would have said that mercy is the oil that runs down from the "head" raised up on the cross; it runs down along the body of the Church to the edges of her robes to those who live on her margins. Where we live in this way, in reciprocal forgiveness and mercy, "the Lord gives his blessing and life forever."

According to Pope Francis in his book *The Name of God is Mercy*:

> Etymologically, "mercy" derives from *misericordis*, which means opening one's heart to wretchedness. And immediately we go to the Lord: mercy is the divine attitude which embraces, it is God's giving himself to us, accepting us and bowing to forgive. Jesus said he came not for those who were good but for the sinners. He did not come for the healthy, who do not need the doctor, but for the sick. For this reason, we can say that mercy is God's identity card (8-9).

According to the ancient Fathers of the Church, the Church herself was born from the wounded side of Christ, when out of his heart there poured out blood and water, symbolic of all the graces of the two chief Sacraments, Baptism and the Eucharist (John 19:34). In short, *Eleos* is God's merciful love poured out upon His people. In the Latin tradition, the principal word for mercy is *Misericordia*, which means, literally "miserable heart." Father George Kosicki, CSB, the great Divine Mercy evangelist, once summed up the meaning of this Latin word as follows: Misericordia means "having a pain in your heart for the pains of others, and taking pains to do something about their pain. "The most comprehensive statement by the Magisterium on the meaning of Divine Mercy can be found in Pope John Paul II's encyclical letter *Dives in Misericordia* (Rich in Mercy, 1981). In that encyclical, the Holy Father made two very important statements about mercy. First, he wrote, "Mercy is love's second name." Secondly, he taught that mercy is "the greatest attribute of God."

I have delved into the etymology of the word *Mercy*. However, these are mere words and somehow these words are distant from us. The word *mercy* finds concrete expression in Jesus, the Incarnate Word. Therefore, as *Misericordiae Vultus* begins,

> Jesus Christ is the face of the Father's mercy. These words might well sum up the mystery of the Christian faith. Mercy has become living and visible in Jesus of Nazareth, reaching its culmination point in him. The Father, "rich in mercy" (Eph 2:4), after having revealed his name to Moses as "a God merciful and gracious, slow to anger, and abounding in steadfast love and faithfulness" (Ex 34:6) has never ceased to show, in various ways throughout history, his divine nature. In the "fullness of time" (Gal 4:4), when everything had been arranged according to his plan of salvation, he sent his only Son into the world, born of the Virgin Mary, to reveal his love for us in a definitive way. Whoever sees Jesus sees the Father (cf. John 14:9). Jesus of Nazareth, by his words, his actions, and his entire person reveals the mercy of God. (*MV*, 1)

The above introductory quote of the Bull of Indiction that brought about the Extraordinary Jubilee Year of Mercy captures the sentiments of this book. Indeed, Jesus is the face of the Father's mercy. This is because Jesus, seeing the crowds of people who followed him, realized that they were tired and exhausted, lost and without a guide, and he felt a deep compassion for them (cf: Matthew 9:36). These very words of the gospel writer re-echo what ministry is all about. Bernadette Farrell in her song "Christ, Be our Light"[1] sums up the dream of Jesus for humanity as regards the ministry of liberation:

> Longing for light, we wait in darkness
> Longing for truth, we turn to You.

---

[1] Christ Be Our Light © 1993, Bernadette Farrell. Published by OCP.

Make us Your own, Your holy people
Light for the world to see.

Christ, be our light!
Shine in our hearts.
Shine through the darkness.
Christ, be our light!
Shine in Your church gathered today.

Longing for peace, our world is troubled
Longing for hope, many despair.
Your word alone has pow'r to save us.
Make us your living voice.

Christ, be our light!
Shine in our hearts.
Shine through the darkness.
Christ, be our light!
Shine in Your church gathered today.

Longing for food, many are hungry
Longing for water, many still thirst.
Make us Your bread, broken for others
Shared until all are fed.

Christ, be our light!
Shine in our hearts.
Shine through the darkness.
Christ, be our light!
Shine in your church gathered today.

If our exercise of ministry would be like that of Jesus, then it must liberate; it must bring liberation to God's people who encounter us. A ministry that truly liberates is a ministry that does not make the one liberated subservient or experience or go through another form of slavery. According to Matthew Kelly in his book: *A Perfect Companion for the Year of Mercy: Beautiful Mercy*:

> On the basis of this compassion..., he healed the sick who were presented to him (cf: Matthew 14:4) and with just some few loaves of bread and fish, he satisfied the enormous crowd (cf: Matthew 15:37). What moved Jesus in all of these situations was nothing other than mercy with which he read the hearts of those he encountered and responded to their deepest need. When he came upon the widow of Nain taking her son out for burial, he felt great compassion for the immense suffering of this grieving mother and gave back her son by raising him from the dead (cf: Luke 7:15). After freeing the demoniac in the country of the Gerasenes, Jesus entrusted him with this mission, "Go home to your friends and tell them how much the Lord has done for you and how he has had mercy upon you (cf: Mark 5:19). The calling of Matthew is also presented within the context of mercy.... (p. 12).

The gospel records many instances in the ministry of Jesus that demonstrated elements of liberation. The story of Jesus' encounter with the blind man Bartimaeus gives us a graphic picture of Jesus' act of compassion when he was on his way to Jerusalem to experience his passion and death. This is what the book seeks to unravel. A truly liberating ministry can only take place effectively within the context of mercy. This is the reason why I find Pope Francis's declaration of the Extraordinary Jubilee Year of Mercy particularly consoling and reassuring. I will make reference to the Bull of Indiction that brought about this extraordinary Jubilee of Mercy, *Misericordiae Vultus,* as I progress in my reflection. A ministry devoid of mercy promotes a culture of death. We must not forget that our eternal life is intrinsically linked to universal Charity: meaning the extent to which we show mercy to others in their moments of vulnerability (Matthew 25). I invite all of us who exercise one ministry or another to take a second look at the demands of ministry and heed the call of Jesus to go and do likewise, for our treatment of the poor and vulnerable is the criterion on which each of us will be judged. Let us renew our commitment to social justice and the betterment of the poor. Pope Francis says:

> We need constantly to contemplate the mystery of mercy. It is a wellspring of joy, serenity, and peace. Our salvation depends on it. Mercy: the word reveals the very mystery of the Most Holy Trinity. Mercy: the ultimate and supreme act by which God comes to meet us. Mercy: the fundamental law that dwells in the heart of every person who looks sincerely into the eyes of his brothers and sisters on the path of life. Mercy: the bridge that connects God and man, opening our hearts to the hope of being loved forever despite our sinfulness. (*MV*, 2)

The above is the motivation for this book. After a serious meditation on all the events of the Year of Mercy, I felt it cannot just pass us by like other equally significant events in the life of the Church like the "Year of Priests," the "Year of the Eucharist," and the like. This book, therefore, is going to be a companion after the Year of Mercy to enable us contemplate the face of God which is mercy. This is because like Pope Francis pointed in *Misericordiae Vultus:* "We need to constantly contemplate the mystery of mercy. It is a wellspring of joy, serenity and peace." I will add that mercy is the very essence of God: His character and identity; God's name is Mercy.

CHAPTER ONE

MINISTRY IS MERCY

"Yes, I believe that this is a time for mercy. The Church is showing her maternal side, her motherly face, to a humanity that is wounded. She does not wait for the wounded to knock on her doors, she looks for them on the streets, she gathers them in, she embraces them, she takes care of them, she makes them feel loved. And so, as I said and I am ever more convinced of it, this is a *Kairos,* our era is a *Kairos* of mercy, an opportune time. When John XXIII solemnly opened the Second Vatican Ecumenical Council, he said, 'The Bride of Christ prefers to use the medicine of mercy rather than arm herself with the weapons of rigor.' ...

"Saint John Paul II took the notion further with his encyclical *Dives in Misericordia,* in which he affirmed that the Church lives an authentic life when it professes and proclaims mercy, the most amazing attribute of the creator and redemptory and when it leads humanity to the font of mercy. In addition, he instituted the festivity of Holy Mercy, endorsed the figure of Saint Faustina Kowalska and focused on Jesus' words on Mercy. Pope Benedict XVI also spoke of this in his teachings: 'Mercy is

> in reality the core of the Gospel message; it is the name of God himself, the face with which he revealed himself in the Old Testament and fully in Jesus Christ, incarnation of Creative and Redemptive Love. This love of mercy also illuminates the face of the Church and is manifested through the Sacraments, in particular that of reconciliation, as well as in works of charity, both of community and individuals. Everything that the Church says and does shows that God has mercy for man.'" (Pope Francis, *The Name of God is Mercy,* pp. 6-7).

In this overview, Pope Francis takes our minds back to documents written by contemporary Popes on the nature of the Church deeply rooted in mercy. The ministry the Church exercises is a ministry of mercy, mercy that permeates every aspect of the Church's life especially in the Church's administration of the Sacraments.

I agree with Pope Francis that ministry is mercy and mercy is ministry when he adds,

> We need to enter the darkness, the night in which so many of our brothers live. We need to be able to make contact with them and let them feel our closeness, without letting ourselves be wrapped up in that darkness and influenced by it...it means trying to reach everyone by sharing the experience of mercy, which we ourselves have experienced, without ever caving into the temptation of feeling that we are just or perfect (p. 67).

The Church is not sending us out there to be judges of one another. We are sent out there to bring healing to a wounded world because we ourselves are wounded, too. For instance, at the end of the Mass when the Church sends us out, we are sent out to witness to the love story we have experienced in the Mass. We are not judges but products of love; yes, we are not judges. The Holy Father continues,

> When a person begins to recognize the sickness in their soul, when the Holy Spirit—the Grace of God—acts within them and moves their hearts towards an initial recognition of their own sins, he needs to find acceptance, not judgment, prejudice or condemnation. He needs to be helped, not pushed away or cast out. Sometimes, when Christians think like scholars of the law, their hearts extinguish that which the Holy Spirit lights up in the heart of a sinner when he stands at the threshold, when he starts to feel nostalgia for God (p. 68).

In the parable of the Wedding Feast in Matthew 22:1-14; Luke 14:15-24, we are presented with the story of people invited to the banquet who turned down the offer at the last minute with excuses and how the master asked the servants to go out into the street and invite anybody they see. Pope Francis asserts that:

> Jesus sends forth his disciples not as holders of power or as masters of a law. He sends them forth into the world asking them to live in the logic of love and selflessness. The Christian message is transmitted by embracing those in difficulty, by embracing the outcast, the marginalized, and the sinner... (p. 93).

Pope Francis writes in *Misericordiae Vultus*, "[I]n the parables devoted to mercy, Jesus reveals the nature of God as that of a father who never gives up until he has forgiven the wrong and overcome rejection with compassion and mercy" (*MV*, 9) The parables to which Pope Francis makes reference are those of the "Lost Sheep, Lost Coin and

Merciful Father (Prodigal Son) (cf: Luke 15:1 - 32). Pope Francis adds, "In these parables, God is always presented as full of joy, especially when he pardons. In them, we find the core of the Gospel and of our faith, because mercy is presented as a force that overcomes everything, filling the heart with Love and bringing consolation through pardon" (*MV*, 9).

The amazing thing about God is that when we have wronged him and he pardons us, he is joyful. Perhaps the one who should be joyful should be the one who experiences God's pardon. Unfortunately, even when we have experienced His mercy, we are still not joyful; we are still moody and as a result we fail to bear witness to God's unfathomable mercy. Anyone who truly encounters or experiences God's mercy cannot but be joyful. This is the kind of mercy St. Augustine experienced and wrote about in his *Confessions* (Book 1, Chapter 18) – the whole concept of indulgence stems from here. Indulgences are various acts of piety, offered by the Church, which the Church claims offer remission of temporal punishment due to forgiven sins in virtue of the merit of Christ and His Church. St. Augustine writes:

> Thou seest all this, O, Lord and dost keep silence- "Long suffering and plenteous in mercy and truth as thou art. Wilt thou keep silence forever? Even now thou drawest from that vast deep silence forever? Even now thou drawest from that vast deep the soul that seeks thee and thirst after thy delight, whose " heart said unto thee, 'I have sought thy face; thy face, Lord, will I seek." for I was far from thy face in the dark shadows of passion. For it is not by our feet, nor by change of place that we either turn from thee or return to thee. That younger son did not charter horses, chariots or ships or fly away on visible

> wings or journey by walking so that in the far country he might prodigally waste all that thou didst give him when he set out. A kind Father when thou gavest; and kinder still when he returned destitute! To be wanton, that is to say, to be darkened, in heart- this is to be far from thy face.

St. Augustine's experience of God's mercy overwhelmed him and he seems to say that the Merciful Father indulges his son, yet when his son came back destitute, he welcomes him with compassion. Sometimes, God indulges us in our selfish desires and our wastefulness just to show how much he loves us.

Pope Francis captures these sentiments succinctly when he writes:

> ...However without a witness to mercy, life becomes fruitless and sterile, as if sequestered in a barren desert. The time has come for the church to take up the joyful call to mercy once more. It is time to return to the basics and to bear the weaknesses and struggles that reawakens us to new life and instills in us the courage to look to the future with hope. (*MV*, 10)

When Jesus saw the crowd of people who followed him, he was moved with pity because they were tired and exhausted. He did not only feed them physically with five loaves of bread and two fish, he healed the sick who were brought to him. This again is beautiful mercy. It is interesting how we can play a part in this compassionate act of Christ by learning from the example of the small boy who brought to Jesus the loaves of bread and fish. The boy demonstrated that mercy is also giving not only receiving; giving even the little we have because Jesus is able to transform it into something greater than we can imagine or think about. This fulfills the dream of Mother Teresa of Calcutta who did the ordinary things in this life extraordinarily. This too is beautiful mercy. It is not so much of the loaves of bread and fish that young man brought to Jesus that is important; but the Love with which he brought it. Thus Pope Francis says:

> The Church's first truth is the love of Christ. The Church makes herself a servant of this love and mediates it to all people; a love that forgives and expresses itself in the gift of oneself. Consequently, wherever the church is present, the mercy of the father must be evident. In our parishes, communities, associations and movements in the world, wherever there are Christians, everyone should find an oasis of mercy. (*MV*, 12)

Perhaps, it is against this backdrop that the Holy Father, Pope Francis, inspired by the Holy Spirit chose as a theme for this extraordinary year of mercy "Merciful Like The Father." In my ardent opinion, the focus is on both the horizontal and vertical relationships: the Horizontal relationship (a relationship between you and your neighbor) takes its source from the vertical relationship (a relationship between man and God). We are called to be merciful towards one another by carrying one another on our shoulders. This can only happen when we are inspired by the merciful act of God towards us; when we have experienced His mercy ourselves. "Nemo dat quod Non Habet": You cannot give what you do not have. Therefore, one can only give mercy who himself has experienced mercy. Who has not experienced the mercy of God or who can claim not to have experienced the mercy of God? Once again, Pope Francis asserts:

> In mercy, we find proof of how God loves us. He gives his entire self, always. Freely, asking nothing in return. He comes to our aid whenever we call upon him. What a beautiful thing that the church begins her daily prayer with the words, "O God, come to my assistance. O Lord, make haste to help me". (Psalm 70:2) The assistance we ask for is already the first of God's mercy towards us. He comes to assist us in our weakness. And His help consists in helping us accept His presence and closeness to us. Day after Day, touched by His compassion, we also can become compassionate towards others. (*MV*, 14).

This experience of mercy is captured in St. Paul's words when he says: "...God proves his love for us in that while we were still sinners, Christ died for us" (Romans 5:8).

Anytime we exercise ministry out of mercy, God is present; the Church is present. Thus mercy-centered ministry is a collaborative one. In other words, one is not alone who exercises ministry out of compassion. There is a multitude of witnesses to this simple but profound act. When Mother Teresa of Calcutta decided to leave the comfort of her religious house to go onto the streets of Calcutta to minister to the homeless, the sick and vulnerable, somehow she knew she was not alone. She knew God was present; she knew the Church was present. In a matter of time, the presence of the Church in her ministry was felt when Pope St. John Paul II requested to see her. Who was mother Teresa of Calcutta that the Holy Father wanted to see her or decided to have audience with her? She is mercy because mercy is beautiful; mercy is evident; mercy cannot be hidden; its radiance is powerful beyond measure. Mercy is Jesus who cannot be hidden under a bushel basket but to be put on a lamp stand for all to see; mercy wins. Mercy is also Jesus who cannot be hidden but hang on the cross as expiation for our sins. Where the Church gathers, mercy is present. You are that Church. The Church subsists in you and so like Mother Teresa, be that light that shines in the darkness of people's life and give hope. The song writer Bernadette Farrell indeed puts it most succinctly when she sings, "Christ be our Light. Shine in our hearts, shine through the darkness. Christ be our light, shine in your Church gathered today."

In our ministry or in the exercise of our ministry, we are called upon to untie the knots that entangle people's lives. Sometimes, you wish you were living in a very huge mansion enjoying all the pleasures of life. Maybe you have witnessed a family living in a very expensive neighborhood, and you see them drive in and out in big cars, and you see yourself fantasizing about what happens in such homes. Yes, the building may be awesome, the cars may be beautiful, but only God knows what is happening in the lives of such people. Sometimes, they carry real burdens, but they have been entombed in their so-called magnificent homes. Our presence in their lives only reveals the knot that has entangled them. Many have been entangled by struggles and anxieties of life, by their weaknesses, failures; some are even at the verge of committing suicide. They need to encounter the mercy of God.

On the other hand, there also those who are not living in big mansions but who need the touch of God's mercy since we are all in need of some wholeness, divine comfort, and a continuous assurance of God's mercy. We are the carriers of such glad tidings like Jesus' encounter with Mary and Martha at the death of Lazarus indicates. We have been entombed like Lazarus, but Jesus wants to free us, and he is asking us like he did ask Martha and Mary, "Do you believe that your brother will rise again?" Jesus is asking us whether we believe he can turn our situations around in our favor. It is within this context of anxiety, pain, and hopelessness that we are called to minister to those in this kind of bondage. St. Paul explains, "When those who follow Jesus seek out the afflicted and comfort them in their misery, they are revealing the very heart of God, who is rich in mercy" (Ephesians 2:4).

To take notice of needs and afflictions is the first step of mercy. To step out of my own needs and my own preoccupation and take notice and then move into another's life with comfort is not only a revelation of the nature of the universe and the God who freely chooses to create it; it is also the key to unlocking God's mercy in our own lives. Jesus taught us, "Blessed are the merciful, for they shall obtain mercy" (Matthew 5:7). So, in addition to bearing witness to the true nature of the universe, acts of mercy open up the floodgates of mercy in our own lives.

BLESSED ARE THE MERCIFUL

The preliminary question is: What does it mean when we say that God is merciful? This simply means when we deserve punishment, God doesn't punish us. He rather blesses us. Mercy is the withholding of a just condemnation. The Bible gives us many illustrations of God's Mercy. And the truth is that God fully demonstrates His Mercy in Jesus Christ. So, in Jesus' Sermon on the Mount, he declared before the crowds: "Blessed are the merciful, for they will be shown mercy." One of Jesus' projects was to make God's people perfect like their Father, and so it was not out of place that He exhorted them to emulate one of the Father's most distinguished attributes - Mercy.

The reality on the ground, however, is that the merciful are abused, taken advantage of and in some cases not shown mercy by others. This means that our world today makes the exercise of mercy extremely difficult. What then did Jesus really mean by declaring that the merciful shall be shown mercy? The merciful in this world are blessed in the sense that they know God's joy. First, the word translated "blessed" is one that has the general meaning of "happy" or "joyful." It is a spiritual blessedness, a divine satisfaction that comes from a right relationship with God. If we are merciful, we are blessed because Mercy is something God Himself displays. God's mercy is the withholding of a just punishment; it is His compassion on the miserable. The more a person starts looking for opportunities to show mercy, the more situations of blessedness he or she will find. Just as man is vulnerable in the face of mercy, God is also vulnerable in the face of mercy. According to Brian Keepers in his Words of Hope post entitled "The Vulnerability of God,"

> By becoming incarnate in Jesus, God makes himself vulnerable to every human experience, including pain and suffering. Nowhere is this vulnerability more on display than in the terrible events of Good Friday. Jesus' flesh torn from being flogged. A twisted crown of thorns and a purple robe to mock him. His body stripped naked. The excruciating agony of a Roman cross. Beyond the physical pain, the brutal act of crucifixion was intended to publicly humiliate and strip a person of all dignity.
>
> We live in a world where people continue to be violated and stripped of dignity, where pain and suffering are a daily reality. The abused child who suffers in silence. The teenage girl sold for sex. The man who is tortured for his faith. The woman who wakes up every morning with chronic pain. In his own suffering and humiliation, Jesus identifies with our suffering and says, "Enough!"
>
> The torture Jesus endured is God's emphatic "No" to all

> violence and suffering; and it's God's "Yes" to the inherent dignity of every human body. It's the triumph of love over hatred, good over evil, forgiveness over sin, life over death. In his atoning sacrifice on the cross, Jesus absorbs all of our suffering and overcomes it. For truly, "by his wounds, we are healed." (April 19, 2019, see https://www.woh.org/devotional/2019/04/19/the-vulnerability-of-god/)

The Holy Father says in the *Misericordiae Vultus*: "On that day, as we seal the Holy Door, we shall be filled, above all, with a sense of gratitude and thanksgiving to the Most Holy Trinity for having granted us an extraordinary time of grace" (5). As Catholic Christians, can we say with all sincerity that it has been an extraordinary time of grace for us? Can we say we have shown mercy just as we have received from the Father? These are serious questions to think about. We should also note that the closing of the Jubilee does not mark the end of God's mercy in our lives. It is like going on a diet to lose some weight. When eventually you succeed, you do not go back to unhealthy eating habits otherwise your dieting would be a complete waste of effort. In the same vein, we are still called to be merciful beyond the Jubilee Year of Mercy that we may obtain mercy ourselves. We should therefore not relent in carrying out the Corporal and Spiritual Works of Mercy in our lives as individuals and Church knowing and believing that we enjoy blessedness by being merciful. May the Lord help us to show the face of His Mercy to others, in season and out of season.

According to Fr. Raniero Cantalamessa O.F.M. CAP in his book *Beatitudes: Eight Steps to Happiness,* "In the Beatitudes, Jesus says 'Blessed are the merciful, for they shall obtain mercy.' The Beatitudes are not an outdated legal code... But a source of perennial inspiration because the one who proclaimed them is risen and alive" (p. 19).

In our exercise of ministry, when mercy is that which animates it, Jesus assures us that we will obtain mercy. The mercy we show people in their moments of vulnerability becomes a catalyst to enable them live their sufferings with purpose. For suffering without purpose leads to despair. Fr. Cantalamessa again says:

> The fifth beatitude in Matthew is 'Blessed are the merciful, for they shall obtain mercy' (Matthew 5:7). Keep in mind that the beatitudes are the self portrait of Christ. We can start by asking this time, "How did Jesus live out mercy? What does life tell us about these beatitudes?"

The word Mercy *(hesed)* has two meanings. The first, according to Fr. Cantalamessa, indicates the attitude of the stronger party in the covenant (God himself) toward the weaker party and is usually expressed by the forgiveness for unfaithfulness and sins. The second meaning indicates the attitude of the need and suffering – not necessarily the sin – of the other and is expressed in what we call works of mercy. There is so to speak, a mercy of the heart and a mercy of hands.

In the ministry of Jesus both aspects of mercy are demonstrated. He heals and He forgives. In other words, Jesus is the visible sign of God's mercy and at the same time he is also moved to compassion for all human suffering and need. This is what the Holy Father calls us to in the Year of Mercy: "Be merciful like the father (Luke 6:36)." This encapsulates man as a potential forgiver and as compassionate towards human suffering. Indeed, in the life of Jesus, both the corporal and the spiritual works of mercy find concrete expression. He feeds the crowd, heals the sick, sets the oppressed free, and even raises the dead (Cf.

Matthew 10:8). He also forgives sins. In Isaiah 53:4, we are told "He took our infirmities and bore our diseases. By His stripes, we are healed."

Reiterating his reflection on mercy, Fr. Cantalamessa OFM. Cap., writes:

> The Primary meaning of mercy in this beatitude is certainly the first, that is the forgiveness and remission of sins. We can assume this from the connection between the beatitude and its reward. "Blessed are the merciful for they shall obtain mercy" points to the mercy of God, who will remit their sins. This statement "Be merciful even as your father is merciful. (Luke 6:36) is immediately clarified in the next verse by this parallel: Forgive and you will be forgiven. (v. 37, p.66)

Jesus Christ amply demonstrated this aspect of mercy namely: forgiveness of sins when, throughout his ministry, he forgave whomever he encountered, the sick, the demon possessed, and the like. Thus, he does not only heal physically, but he heals spiritually by forgiving sins. The healing of the paralytic (Matthew 9:2-8) is one example of the relationship between the Sacrament of Reconciliation and the Sacrament of the Anointing of the Sick. The more the Pharisees and the scribes accused him of entertaining sinners, the more Jesus kept welcoming them. For He says "I came not to call the righteous but sinners. (Mark 2: 17). Every sinner feels welcome in Jesus' presence not because he condones sins but as Fr. Cantalamessa puts it, "Feeling themselves accepted by Him and not judged, sinners listened to Him willingly" (p. 60).

Mercy is just. In other words, justice demands that we show mercy. Anyone who fails to show mercy has violated the cardinal virtue of Justice. The reason why like the

Pharisees many of us cannot show mercy is the fact that we have our own vision or we have set our own standards as regards who sinners are and that anyone who does not fall within this standard is labeled or branded a sinner and is condemned. Again, Fr. Cantalamessa writes,

> The Pharisees had their vision of the law and of what conformed to or contradicted it and they considered as reprobates all those who did not conform to their practices. Jesus does not deny that sin and sinners exist, he does not justify the fraud of Zacchaeus or the adultery of the woman. The fact that he refers to them as "those who are sick" (Mark 2: 17) proves that what Jesus condemns is people's establishing what true righteousness is on their own and considering everyone else, thieves, unrighteous and adulterers" (Luke 18:11), denying even the possibility of their changing.

The parable of the Pharisee and the publican or tax collector brings to the fore strongly what Jesus wishes to communicate to us all: "He also told this parable to some who trusted in themselves that they are righteous and despised others (Luke 18:9-14):

> Two men went up to the temple to pray, one a Pharisee and the other a Tax Collector. The Pharisee, standing by himself, was praying thus, "God, I thank you that I am not like other people: thieves, rogues, adulterers, or even like this tax collector. I fast twice a week; I give a tenth of all my income." But the tax collector, standing far off, would not even look up to heaven, but was beating his breast and saying, "God be merciful to me, a sinner!" I tell you, this man went down to his home justified rather than the other; for all who exalt themselves will be

humbled, but all who humble themselves will be exalted.

Fr. Cantalamessa adds, "According to one exegete, 'Jesus, in other words, was more critical of those who dismissively condemned "sinners" than the sinners themselves" (p.67). We have a God who delights in showing mercy. Jesus, therefore, who is the only begotten son of God naturally, assumes this nature of his Father from whom every good and perfect gift comes (James 1:17). Anytime, Jesus performs a merciful act, he is indirectly telling us that "[t]his is the way my father acts" and this is the way to go. Anytime we fail to show mercy, we should ask ourselves whether this is how Jesus will act. If we are seeking to show mercy to holy people, then we will never be able to show mercy. The fact that God shows mercy is characteristic of Him. God says "I desire mercy, not sacrifice" (Hosea 6:6, Matthew 9:13). In Psalm 130, the Psalmist says, "If You O Lord should mark our guilt, Lord who will survive; For with You is found forgiveness and for this we revere You".

We revere God most importantly because He continually shows us Mercy. Again, in Psalm 136, we have a litany of mercy attributes given to God. It says "For His mercy endures forever":

O give thanks to the Lord, for he is good,
for his steadfast love endures forever.
O give thanks to the God of gods,
for his steadfast love endures forever
O give thanks to the Lord of lords,
for his steadfast love endures forever
who alone does great wonders
for his steadfast love endures forever;
who by understanding made the heavens,
for his steadfast love endures forever...

Therefore, the Holy Father's call on us during the Extraordinary Jubilee Year of Mercy to be merciful like the Heavenly Father shows that "being merciful seems to be an essential quality for a human being if he or she is to reflect the image and likeness of God (see Genesis 1:26). Be merciful, even as your father is merciful. (Luke 6:36) is a paraphrase of the famous verse, "You shall be holy; for I the Lord your God am holy." (Leviticus 10:2).

The joy that fills the heart of God when he forgives us finds expression in the statement that "The angels in heaven rejoice over one repentant sinner than over ninety-nine righteous people." In the parables of the lost sheep, lost coin, and merciful father (prodigal son), we see joy expressed as a consequence of mercy. In any case, the parable of the Prodigal son is only one of three parables in Lk 15 that we are very familiar with. In Lk 15, three things get lost. A sheep, a coin, and a son. But these things do not get lost the same way. A sheep gets lost and is conscious that it is lost. It can bleat but cannot find its way home. The shepherd must come and find it. The coin gets lost differently. When a coin is lost, it does not know that it is lost. Another must sweep the room and come find it. But when a man gets lost, he knows he is lost, and he must also come to his senses and find his way back home himself. I think that some men represent both the lost sheep and the lost coin. They get lost and they cannot find their way home because they cannot do that on their own. Therefore, the lack of knowledge of being lost is from the fact that they have become one with the lost land. It is difficult to find a coin when it rusts.

I mentioned that three things get lost in Lk 15 and all three get found. The joy that accompanies the finding is so intense because in all these the one who goes looking for the item does a diligent search. That is why I love one of the songs of Kirk Franklin, "My Life Is In Your Hands," in which the artist sings that joy comes in the morning but troubles don't last always.

In reality, there is a fourth thing that gets lost in Lk 15. The fourth thing is the elderly son. The tragedy of Lk 15 is that while we are assured that the sheep, the coin, and the prodigal son are each found, there is no assurance that the elder son was ever found. Did he eventually go back into the house to join his younger brother? Was his father able to convince him to return? Jesus ends the parable with no answer. Getting found is not automatic. At the end of the day, we have a choice. The father can have his arms wide open, but if we refuse to make a return, no amount of compassion can help us. Our desire to be joyful is a choice. Just as God is joyful whenever he shows us mercy, joy will also be the portion of the one who shows mercy. If you fail to show mercy, joy will elude you.

Joy, according Matthew Kelly in his *A Call to Joy: Living in the Presence of God,* "is not simply a feeling of happiness. Joy is the all – intoxicating feeling of becoming. It is the greatest of emotional and spiritual sensations. We experience joy when we grow, and we grow when we live in the presence of God and listen to the promptings of the Holy Spirit" (p. 33).

Pope Francis says of the Parable of the Prodigal Son:

> Every confessor must accept the faithful as the father in the parable of the prodigal son: a father who runs out to meet his son despite the fact that he has squandered away his inheritance. Confessors are called to embrace the repentant son who comes back home and to express the joy of having him back again. Let us never tire of also going out to the other son who stands outside, incapable of rejoicing in order to explain to him that his judgment is severe and unjust and meaningless in the light of the

father's boundless mercy (*MV*, 17).

We tend to condemn the attitude of the 'elder son.' But he represents a humanity that is hurting and wounded and needs healing. Perhaps, he is not jealous as we think, but he is perhaps scandalized by the merciful attitude of his father. He is overwhelmed and astonished at his father's love. Like the elder son, we often think that sinners are not worthy of God's love because their sins are so heavy. Therefore, we expect God who is a consuming fire to destroy them and we are disappointed when he shows mercy instead. The Holy Father says we must go out there and look for them because they need us. More importantly in these trying times of the Church's life in which people are hurting and wounded because of scandal and abuse in Church leadership, there are those who think priests and bishops involved in this do not deserve God's mercy.

There are other instances in the scriptures when God is presented as one who is joyful when he pardons. In Ezekiel 33:11, God says "I have no pleasure in the death of the wicked, but I take pleasure that the wicked turns from his ways and live." The word "pleasure" can be substituted with the word "Joy". Again, in Micah 7:18, He says, "God delights in mercy." I am just imagining how the lost sheep felt when the shepherd found it. I can just picture it dancing as the shepherd carried it home on his shoulders. The fact that the shepherd did not castigate it or condemn it but joyfully carried it upon his shoulders gave hope to the lost sheep. Also, the fact that the merciful father in the parable of the prodigal son welcomed his wayward son with joy after his returning destitute and the fact that the woman found the lost coin in her room after going through a long arduous search and runs to tell her neighbors that she had found her lost coin should give hope to every sinner. The reason why we should be hopeful is the fact that God is merciful. This is what the Church calls us to when the Holy Father proclaimed the Extraordinary Jubilee Year of Mercy.

We have received so much from God. It is our turn to give others the opportunity and reason to be joyful and hopeful. In the book of the prophet Micah, God expressed human emotions, and this revealed him as an anthropomorphic God:

> Hear then, what the Lord says, arise, present your plea before the mountains, and let the hills hear your voice! Hear, O mountains, the plea of the Lord, pay attention, O foundations of the earth! For the Lord has a plea against his people and he enters into trial with Israel. O my people, what have I done to you or how have I wearied you? Answer me! For I brought you up from the Land of Egypt; from the place of slavery. I released you; and I sent before you Moses, Aaron and Miriam. My people, remember what Moab's king, Balak planned, and how Balaam, the son of Beor, answered him from Shittim to Gilgal, that you may know the just deeds of the Lord. With what shall I come before the Lord, and bow before God the Most High? Shall I come before him with holocausts and with calves a year old? Will the Lord be pleased with thousands of rams, with myriads streams of oil? Shall I give my first born for my crime, the fruit of my body for the sins of my soul? You have been told, O man, what is good, and what the Lord require of you; only to do the right and to love goodness, and to walk humbly with your God (Micah 6:1 – 8).

God is not interested in the myriad of sacrifices and holocausts that we bring to him every day when it does not translate into how kindly we deal with one another. Indeed, justice demands that we show mercy. When you show someone mercy, remember that you are not doing the person a favor; rather, your capacity for showing mercy is a privilege; a privilege in participating in God's love. Showing mercy to someone is an automatic ticket to heaven because your heavenly father is merciful to those who show mercy.

I remember a song we used to sing in the seminary entitled "And the Father would dance" as found in the book of the prophet Zephaniah in which he presents God as a father who dances and exults over his children who decide to return to him, who decide to repent. Can you imagine God dancing over you a sinner because by His grace you have decided to repent and go back home? Instead of condemning us, He went in search of us:

> Shout for joy, O daughter of Zion. Sing joyfully, O Israel! Be glad and exult with all your heart, o daughter of Jerusalem! The Lord has removed the judgment against you. On that day, it shall be said of Jerusalem: fear not, O Zion, be not discouraged, the Lord your God is in your midst, a mighty savior! He will rejoice over you with gladness, and renew you in His love. He will sing joyfully because of you, as one sings at festivals (Zephaniah 3:14 – 18).

According to Fr. Cantalamessa, "But why, we can ask, should one sheep count as much as all the remaining sheep put together, and the one that counts most should be the one that has gotten lost and created the most problems?" I have found a convincing explanation in the poet Charles Peguy: "being lost, this sheep," like the younger son, made God's heart tremble. God feared losing him forever, being forced to condemn him and be deprived of him for eternity. This fear caused hope to arise in God, and once that hope was realized, "And this (person's) very repentance /was for Him (God), the crowning of a hope...."

For human beings, what makes hope possible is the fact that we do not know the future and, therefore, we hope. For God, who knows the future, what makes hope possible is that He does not want to and in a certain sense cannot - bring to pass what He wants without our consent. The free will of human beings explains the existence of hope in God.

CHAPTER TWO

SHOULD NOT YOU HAVE HAD MERCY ON YOUR FELLOW SERVANT AS I HAD MERCY ON YOU (MATTHEW 18:33)

Mercy is generosity. The very core of Christianity is not the focus on self but the forgetfulness of self and the focus on the other, says Fr. Lamy Richards. The Parable that Jesus uses to illustrate the need for us to be merciful to others because God has been merciful to all of us, too, is critical to our understanding of the Clarion call of the Holy Father, in the recently-ended Extraordinary Jubilee Year of Mercy to carry one another on our shoulders. The Logo of the Year of Mercy simply attests to this fact. All have sinned and fallen short of the glory of God. To be merciful toward each other is the will of God for humanity. Therefore, I wish to place the text in its proper context. "It is not the will of your heavenly father that one of these little ones be lost." (Mt 18:14)

By this verse, God desires that all of us be saved. He is a God of another chance. In the same way, he desires that we give each other another chance; we should complement each other's effort to enter heaven. He is quick to forgive us our sins. This is His nature. He does not hold our sins against us. Therefore, having been created in the image and likeness of God, we should also be quick to forgive each other. That is why he says that even if you are the one who has been wronged, take the initiative and reconcile with your offender. Since forgiveness is difficult, Peter wanted to justify himself and so he asked Jesus, "Lord, if my brother sins against me, how often must I forgive him? As many as seven times?" Jesus answered, "I say to you, not seven times but seventy - seven times. Realizing that the disciples were still not clear with His teaching on forgiveness; Jesus told them the parable of the unforgiving servant.

Jesus told Peter and his brothers:

> That is why the kingdom of heaven may be likened to a king who decided to settle accounts with his servants. When he began the accounting, a debtor was brought before him who owed him a huge amount. Since he had no way of paying it back, his master ordered him to be sold along with his wife, his children and all his property in payment of the debt. At that, the servant fell down, did him homage and said, "Be patient with me and I will pay you back in full." Moved with compassion, the master of the servant let him go and forgave him the loan. When that servant had left, he found one of his fellow servants who owed him a much smaller amount. He seized him and started to choke him, demanding, "Pay back what you owe me." Falling to his knees, his fellow servant begged him, "Be patient with me, and I will pay you back." But he refused. Instead, he had him put in prison until he paid him back the debt. Now when his fellow servants saw what had happened, they were deeply disturbed and went to their master and reported the whole affair. His master summoned him and said to him "You wicked servant, I forgave you your entire debt because you begged me to. Should you not have had pity on your fellow servant, as I had pity on you?" Then in

> anger, his master handed him over to the torturers until he paid back the whole debt. So will my heavenly father do to you unless each of you forgives his brother from his heart. (Matthew 11:23-35)

Jesus' answer to Peter's question: "How many times must he forgive his brother?" shows that what is demanded of the disciples is limitless forgiveness. The difference between the debt the servant owed his master and the debt his fellow servant owed him was enormous and brings out the absurdity of the conduct of the servant who had received the greater pardon from his master and yet refused to forgive the little debt that his fellow servant owed him. "Then in anger his master handed him over to the torturers until he should pay back the whole debt" (Matthew 18:34). By the above statement of the master, since the debt is so great as to be unpayable, the punishment will be endless. The father's forgiveness already given would be withdrawn at the final judgment for those who have not imitated the forgiving act of the Merciful Father.

Again, there is a further reason why our forgiveness must be limitless. The reason of the celebration of the Sabbath according to Deuteronomy 5:15 is precisely the fact that God freed Israel from bondage. It would stand to reason that no one can be held in debt on the Sabbath. The Sabbath guarantees freedom. No one can be perpetually in debt in Israel. If we read carefully Jesus's reply to Peter, Jesus says "I do not say to you seven times but seventy times seven." That would be 490 times. That is not just a mathematical number. The number 49 is seven times seven. That is the beginning of the Jubilee Year (the 50th) which Leviticus 25 talks about. It is the year in which captives are released, and those who are in debt have their debts cancelled. Jesus requires of Peter a complete Jubilee and total freedom of whoever might be indebted to us. Rev. Fr. Michael Mensah, in his book *Breaking the Word* asserts:

> That is precisely the reason why the parable speaks about debts. Let us say one thing about it. A denarius was a day's wage. A talent according to some scholars, was about 10,000 denarii. The man owed 10,000 talents. OK that is 100,000,000 denarii. That's how many days he would have to work to pay his debt (approximately 250,000 years). It was an impossible debt to pay. Then he goes to throttle a fellow servant who owed him 100 denarii (3 months salary). Jesus' point is that the kind of debt we owe is not the type we can ever pay. It can only be paid by the exercise of the "sabbatical" law of the remission of debts. And that law binds everyone without exception. (p. 247)

What struck me in this parable is the fact that it was the other servants who saw the wickedness of this servant who had been forgiven much and yet failed to forgive his fellow servant. Sometimes, our attitude as Christians causes a scandal to other Christians, and what is more appalling is that we cannot even forgive our fellow Christians. You can imagine what scandal we cause pagans. We attend the same church, receive communion together, but at the least provocation, we are at each other's throat and unwilling to forgive. Anyone who fails to forgive is a captive and needs to be freed. Captives cannot free themselves. We need to lighten the loads of unforgiveness in our lives. If you are struggling to forgive, just take a leap of faith and allow the mercy of God to convict you to repentance.

Again, the parable, according to Pope Francis,

> contains a profound teaching for all of us: 'Jesus affirms

> that mercy is not only an action of the father; it becomes a criterion for ascertaining who His true children are. In short, we are called to show mercy because mercy has first been shown to us. Pardoning offences becomes the clearest expression of merciful love, and for us Christians it is an imperative from which we cannot excuse ourselves. At times, how hard it seems to forgive! And yet, pardon is the instrument placed into our fragile hands to attain serenity of heart. To let go of anger, wrath, violence and revenge are necessary conditions to living joyfully. Let us therefore heed the Apostle's exhortation: 'Do not let the sun go down on your anger' (Ephesians 4:26). Above all, let us listen to the words of Jesus who made mercy an idea of life and a criterion for the credibility of our faith: "Blessed are the merciful, for they shall obtain mercy". (Matthew 5:7). (*MV*, 9).

As the pope concludes, we should particularly aspire to live the beatitudes in our daily lives. To live out the beatitudes meaningfully, I propose to you the various ministries in the Church that can be practical avenues for proper Christian living.

THE VARIOUS MINISTRIES IN THE CHURCH AND THEIR FUNCTIONS IN THE LIGHT OF MERCY

Mercy permeates every aspect of the Church's life and mission. The Sacraments and the various ministries in the Church are the well spring of mercy. Pope Francis says:

> Mercy is the very foundation of the Church's life. All of her pastoral activity should be caught up in the tenderness she makes present to believers; nothing in her preaching and in her witness to the world can be lacking

in mercy. The Church's very credibility is seen in how she shows merciful compassionate love. The Church 'has an endless desire to show mercy'. (*MV*, 10)

In the midst of wars, tensions in our families and the scandals that have hit the Church in recent times, the Church (the Body of Christ) that is wounded is at the same time a Church that must heal, for as the Holy Father quotes Saint John Paul II in his *Dives in Misericordia*,

> The Church lives an authentic life when she professes and proclaims mercy- the most stupendous attribute of the Creator and of the Redeemer and when she brings people close to the sources of the savior's mercy, of which she is the trustee and dispenser. (*MV*, 11)

2.1 Definition of Ministry

According to the Catechism of the Church, Christ is himself the source of ministry in the Church. He gave her authority and mission, orientation and goal:

> In order to shepherd the people of God and to increase its numbers without cease, Christ the Lord set up in his Church a variety of offices which aim at the good of the whole body. The holders of office, who are invested with sacred power, are in fact, dedicated to promoting the interests of their brethren, so that all who belong to the People of God may attain salvation. (*CCC*, 874)

In the Catholic Church the term **'Minister'** enjoys a variety of usages. It most commonly refers to the person, whether lay or ordained, who is commissioned to perform some act on behalf of the Church. It is not a particular office or rank of clergy, as is the case in some other churches, but **'Minister'** may be used as a collective term for vocational or professional pastoral leaders including clergy (bishops, deacons, priests) and non-clergy (theologians and lay ecclesial ministers). It is also used in reference to the canonical and liturgical administration of sacraments, as part of some offices, and with reference to the exercise of the apostolate.

Ministry is simply the exercising of the Priesthood we share in Christ. This is what Vatican II (1963 -1965) calls the Church to. The full, conscious, and active participation of all in the Liturgy has been the prime concern of all Catholic Parishes. The Church wants us to realize that the Mass, particularly, is a public worship of the Christian community, not in competition with other devotion like Rosary, Novenas and the like.

To minister is to serve. In scripture, Jesus testified that he came to serve, not to be served and to give his life as a ransom for many. In several of Paul's Letters, he captured this vision of Jesus, developed it, and applied it to the daily life of the early Christians and Vocations in the Church. Paul saw clearly that this was what Jesus intended his Church to be namely a community of believers in which each member with his or her own unique gifts all working together (ministering) to build up the Body of Christ, the Church (Cf. 1 Corinthians 12:4-21). Indeed, ministry is about people, and so any activity that would promote the common good is ministry.

In this area of the Church, Vatican II has developed the idea of the ministry in a beautiful way. The Council has reminded us that we all share in the one priesthood of Christ: the faithful attain this ministry through baptism, and the ordained Priest or Deacon through Holy Orders. Therefore, we are a priestly people. As scripture puts it beautifully, "You are chosen race, a royal Priesthood, a holy nation, God's own people, in order that you may proclaim the mighty acts of Him who called you out of darkness into His marvelous light" (1 Peter 2:9).

2.2 Various Ministries in the Church

Scripturally, various passages utilize the language of servant (ministry) to indicate those charged with spiritual functions or pastoral care of the community: **(1 Corinthians 4: 1 - 2; Hebrews 8: 2; Matthew 20:26, etc).**

Specific distinction in terminology may be found in various documents, among others: Participation of the Lay Faithful in the Clerical Ministry can be put under the following headings:

1. **Lay Ministers**
2. **Ecclesial Ministers**
3. **Sacramental Ministers**
4. **Instituted Ministers**

In a general sense, any Christian exercising ministry is a minister. Since all the baptized are part of the universal priesthood, whenever they engage in their vocation to evangelize the world and to help those in need, they are ministers.

In addition, the Church calls people to the responsible stewardship of their time and talent in support of the Church. This often takes the form of volunteering for the specific lay ministry, most of which are liturgical, catechetical or involved in pastoral care and social justice.

Liturgical lay ministries include lectors who proclaim

scriptural passages during the Eucharistic celebration, altar servers and acolytes, who assist the presider at the altar, cantors and music ministers who lead the singing, extraordinary ministers of the Holy Communion who serve during Mass and /or who take Holy Communion to the sick and homebound, and ushers or ministers of hospitality who direct the seating and procession of the assembly.

Catechetical lay ministers include catechists (Children Service Animators and teachers at Catholic Schools), dismissal leaders (ministers who lead RCIA catechumens on Sundays), retreat leaders, youth group leaders. Other lay ministries include those who work with charitable organizations (St. Vincent de Paul Society), pastoral care and outreach, or advocacy for social justice.

Ecclesial Ministers include those within the Church who are called by God and the assembly to serve as ministers to the whole people of God. These people respond to this vocation by receiving the proper formation, usually including graduate studies in theology or divinity, and then exercising some leadership role in the community. In common usage, when someone refers to a "minister of the church" they are referring to any one of these "professional" ministers.

The Catholic Church identifies five ecclesial vocations, three of which are ordained. Theologians and lay ecclesial ministers are not necessarily ordained, while bishops, presbyters and deacons are ordained. While only the latter are considered clergy by the Catholic Church, all are considered ministers in the professional and vocational sense.

Sacramental Ministers include those who administer a sacrament, meaning that they are a conduit of sacramental grace. This is not an office or position but instead a function that different kinds of people may perform, depending on the sacrament. There are two kinds of ministers in this sense. The ordinary minister of a sacrament has both the spiritual power to perform the sacrament (i.e. a valid sacrament) and the canonical authority to perform the sacrament (i.e. a licit sacrament).

By way of example, the priest is the only minister of the Eucharist. If a priest is, for some reason, debarred and yet still celebrates the Eucharist, he does so illicitly (i.e. against Canon Law) but the Eucharist is still valid. However, in terms of the sacraments of Catholic marriage and Reconciliation (the Sacrament of Penance), although the priest is the ordinary minister, he must have permission from the appropriate authority if he is to celebrate these sacraments validly.

An extraordinary minister has the spiritual power but may only perform the sacrament in certain special instances under canon law. If an extraordinary minister performs a sacrament illicitly, the sacrament is effective but the person ministering could be liable for an ecclesiastical penalty, such as an interdict. By way of example, an extraordinary minister of Holy Communion who is authorized to bring Holy Communion within a particular parish or diocese but takes it to someone outside of the authorized area, acts illicitly, but the person still receives Holy Communion and all the benefits that come with it. If a person who is not an ordinary minister attempts to celebrate certain sacraments, it is considered to be invalid. The above kinds of ministries have different functions. Therefore, no one can usurp another's authority or ministry to his advantage. There are proper channels for the exercise of ministry and so every member of the Church must be educated to know the extent to which one exercises ministry.

The various ministries in the Church are meant to help realize the mission of the Church which is primarily evangelization. Anything apart from this is a misplaced priority. The aim of ministry can be summed up in Jesus' last words to his disciples: "Therefore go and make disciples of all nations, baptizing them in the name of the Father and of the son and of the Holy Spirit, and teaching them to obey everything I have commanded you. And surely, I am with you always, to the very end of the age. (Matthew 28: 19 - 20).

"The Church on earth is by its nature is missionary, since according to the plan of the Father, it has its origin in the mission of the Son and the Holy Spirit" 4. The various ministries of the Church are the means by which the Laity participates in the mission of the Church. Every Christian receives this mandate by virtue of his or her baptism. "Evangelization is the special grace and vocation of the Church. It is her essential function.." The Decree on the Apostolate of Lay People puts it beautifully when it says:

> ...In the organism of a living body no member plays a purely passive part, sharing in the life of the body it shares at the same time in its activity. This is true for the body of Christ, the Church: "the whole body achieves full growth in dependence on the full functioning of each part"6 (Ephesians 4:16). It continues that "Between the members of the body there exists, further, such a unity and solidarity (cf. Ephesians 4: 16) that a member who does not work at the growth of the body to the extent of his possibilities must be considered useless to both the church and himself.

In Jesus' very last word to His disciples, He gave Christian ministers and ministries four major objectives. We can then sum up the words of the Great Commission in the following words: "Shepherd the people: "Jesus said, "Take care of my sheep" (John 21: 16). "Keep watch over yourselves and all the flock of which the Holy Spirit has made you overseers. Be shepherds of the Church of God, which he bought with His own blood" (Acts 20: 28). Be a spiritual watchman. "Obey your leaders and submit to their authority. They watch over you as men who must give an account. Obey them so that their work will be a joy, not a burden, for that would be of no advantage to you" (Hebrew 13: 17). Teach the Word of God: "Go, stand in the temple courts ..and tell the people the full message of this new life" (Acts 5: 20).

But the work of ministry is not just to be done by ministers and Christian ministries. All Christians are all called to serve. "For we are God's workmanship, created in Christ Jesus to do good works, which God prepared in advance for us to do" (Ephesians 2: 10). "It was he who gave some to be apostles, some to be prophets, some to be evangelists, and some to be pastors and teachers" (Ephesians 4: 11). That is just the beginning of the ways we might be used to carrying out the ministry of God. Some people have their ministry in music, others with children, some to specific groups like the chemically dependent or to prisoners, but everyone has a spot to minister. For everyone, the objective of ministry is the same - to save as many as possible for the Kingdom of God before Christ returns. The Bible says it in many different ways, but the message is always the same. The ultimate objective of ministry I believe is salvation. The 1983 Code Canon Law confirms this when it says that "The Supreme Law of the Church is the salvation of souls (1752). "The Lord is not slow in keeping His promise, as some understand slowness. He is patient with us, not wanting anyone to perish, but everyone to come to repentance" (2 Peter 3:9).

From the above explanation of ministry, it is obvious that in the exercise of our different ministries, we should all bear in mind that all have a common objective namely the salvation of souls. Therefore, under no circumstances must one think that his ministry is better than the others. Our work is a collaborative one. "Consequently, the mission of the Church must be sought in the mission of Christ himself"

CHAPTER THREE

A PRIEST TO TURN TO: BLIND BARTIMAEUS' ENCOUNTER WITH JESUS (MARKS 10:46-52).

> They came to Jericho. And as he was leaving Jericho with his disciples and a sizable crowd, Bartimaeus, a blind man, the son of Timaeus, sat by the roadside begging. On hearing that it was Jesus of Nazareth, he began to cry out and say, "Jesus son of David, have pity on me." And many rebuked him telling him to be silent. But he kept calling out all the more, "Son of David have pity on me." Jesus stopped and said, "call him." So they called the blind man, saying to him, "Take courage; get up, he is calling you.' He threw aside his cloak, sprang up and came to Jesus. Jesus said to him in reply, "What do you want me to do for you?" The blind man replied to him, "Master, I want to see." Jesus told him, "Go your way; your faith has saved you." Immediately he received his sight and followed him on his way.

The story of Jesus' encounter with the blind man Bartimaeus is exactly God's vision for humankind namely that we should not forget the vulnerable in our society. In the front cover page of my book, you will find the picture depicting Jesus' encounter with the Blind Man Bartimaeus.

This encounter reveals to all and sundry the kind of priest one should turn to and how as ministers we have the onerous task to minister to people even in awkward circumstances. The story is set within the wider context of Jesus final journey from Jericho to Jerusalem where death awaits him. Perhaps, that was the moment he should be pre-occupied with misery and anguish because his death is imminent. Also, the crowd following him was so thick for him to think about someone like Bartimaeus, a man at the margins of society. Bartimaeus was too insignificant to be noticed by anyone with more important commitment and pre-occupation like Jesus. It may look absurd at first to think that Jesus will waste his time on someone like Bartimaeus when death awaits him. But it is in this bizarre situation that Jesus bore authentic witness to mercy. We too who are in ministry can easily forget ourselves in ministering to people often at the margins of society. But this is what Jesus will not ignore as these moments really demonstrate God's unfailing compassion for all even in obscure circumstances. Pope Francis, reflecting on this story says:

> ... let us consider the different reaction of bishops, priests, sisters, seminarians, to the cries we hear or fail to hear. It is as if the evangelist wanted to show us the effect which Bartimaeus' cry had on people's lives, on the lives of Jesus' followers. How did they react when faced with the suffering of that man on the side of the road, who no one takes any notice of, who receives no more than a gesture of almsgiving, who is wallowing in his misery and who is not part of the group following the Lord (99)?

These questions that Pope Francis raises are fundamental and relevant questions that are worth reflecting on as we exercise our various ministries. They are questions that border on the self-centeredness, selfishness, egotistic and individualistic tendencies that represent the 21st century society. There is always the tendency to focus on the powerful and rich at the expense of the poor and vulnerable. The poor and the marginalized like blind Bartimaeus have been rejected by society but they always remain hopeful that someday their story will change. Having been rejected by society, they wish to come to Jesus, hoping to find solace. Here too they experience rejection and discrimination. That is the more reason why we have to pay attention to them. There were three responses to the cry of the blind man and these responses are still relevant today for effective ministry: "Pass by", "Be quiet," "Take heart and get up." The Holy Father expatiates on these phrases and I wish to adopt them for our consideration.

THEY PASSED BY

The Holy Father says:

> Some of those who passed by Bartimaeus did not even hear him shouting. They were with Jesus, they looked at Jesus, they wanted to hear him. But they were not listening. Passing by is the response of indifference, of avoiding other people's problems because they do not affect us. It is not my problem. We do not hear them, we do not recognize them. Deafness. Here we have the temptation to see suffering as something natural, to take injustice for granted. And yes, there are people like that: I am here with God, with my consecrated life, chosen by God for ministry and yes, it is normal that there are those who are sick, poor, suffering and it is so normal that I no longer notice the cry for help. To become accustomed. We say to ourselves, "This is nothing unusual; things were

> always like this, as long as it does not affect me." It is the response born of a blind, closed heart, a heart which has lost the ability to be touched and hence the possibility to change... (99-100).

Our culture is one of apathy towards the sufferings of others. No one can give an excuse for not seeing the suffering of others. In fact, the crowd following Jesus cannot claim that they did not see Bartimaeus. He has always been there and sometimes a few dropped coins into his bowl. May be the real blind people are the crowd following Jesus not Bartimaeus who could see Jesus with his heart. The Holy Father intimated that "To pass by, without hearing the pain of our people, without sinking roots in their lives and in their world, is like listening to the word of God without letting it take root and bear fruit in our hearts. Like a tree, a life without roots is one which withers and dies" (101).

BE QUIET

"Be quiet" was the response of the crowd to Bartimaeus when he started shouting. How come now they recognize him when he started shouting? I thought the crowd took no notice of him. Perhaps, the scolding of Bartimaeus by those who think they have the right to be with Jesus is the attitude of some Christians today. A Christian family hires the services of a maid. They burden her with all the family chores to the extent that even on Sundays that the family leaves for Church, she is left at home to go through the drudgery of cleaning the house and preparing food for the family. In this instance, the family demonstrate that they have the right to be with Jesus and not that poor maid. This attitude of the Christian Family is what the Holy Father describes as:

> ... the drama of the isolated consciousness, of those disciples who think that the life of Jesus is only for those who deserve it. There is an underlying contempt for the faithful people of God: "This blind man who has to interfere with everything, let him stay where he is." They seem to believe there is only room for the "worthy", for the "better people," and little by little they separate themselves, become distinct, from others. They have made their identity a badge of superiority. That identity which makes itself superior is no longer proper to the pastor but rather to a foreman... (101-102).

For our ministry to be fruitful we must drop the cloak of prejudice, superiority and contentment and embrace a commitment to restoring dignity to people who have lost it through injustice and harsh economic realities.

TAKE HEART AND GET UP

Sometimes our very words can be a source of shame for us. Now, they recognize him now that Jesus called for him. The highest level of hypocrisy is when we pretend not to recognize the sufferings of those around us and all of a sudden, they come to the lime light and we forget so easily about how we treated them in the past. In many instances in many nations of the world, we hear of the sufferings of people and when they encounter a more humane person who changes their destiny, the spotlight is put on them especially by the media. Every media person wants to grant interview to such a person. Hypocrisy. Jesus led and showed the way to go and that is the example he set for all ministers. We must pay attention to everyone especially those neglected by society. We must remember the Church's preferential option for the poor. The Holy Father says:

> Unlike those who simply passed by, the gospel says that Jesus stopped and asked what was happening. "What is happening here?" Who is making noise?" He stopped when someone cried out to him. He singled him out from the nameless crowd and got involved in his life. And far from ordering him to keep quiet, he asked him, "Tell me, what do you want me to do for you?" Jesus didn't have to show that he was different, somehow apart, and he didn't give the beggar a sermon; he didn't decide whether Bartimaeus was worthy or not before speaking to him. He simply asked him a question, looked at him and sought to come into his life, to share his lot. And by doing this he gradually restored the man's lost dignity, the man who was on the side of the path and blind; Jesus included him. Far from looking down on him, Jesus was moved to identify with the man's problems and thus to show the transforming power of mercy. There can be no compassion and I mean compassion without stopping (103-104).

Indeed, the Holy Father hit the nail right there on the head when he says that there cannot be compassion without stopping. The parable of the Good Samaritan is a case in point. The Good Samaritan stopped got down from his horse, got down to the man who fell to robbers, poured oil and wine on his wounds put him on his horse and virtually dragged the horse on which the wounded man laid to an inn. Not only that, he spent the night there, paid for the bills and was ready to pay more when the need arises. This is compassion with a difference. This is what Jesus invites us to. The Priest and Levite who ignored the man who fell to the robbers represent the crowd in the story and indeed all of us who ignore people in the daily exercise of our ministries. Pope

Francis says again: "If you do not stop, you do not suffer with him, you do not have divine compassion. There is no "compassion" that does not listen and show solidarity with the other. Compassion is not about zapping, it is not about silencing pain, it is about the logic of love, of suffering with. A logic, a way of thinking and feeling, which is not grounded in fear but in the freedom born of love and of desire to put the good of others before all else. A logic born of not being afraid to draw near to the pain of our people. Even if often this means no more than standing at their side and praying with them" (104). The result of Jesus' compassion towards Bartimaeus was that he became a disciple of Jesus. We are told that immediately he received healing, he threw off his cloak and followed Jesus. How many opportunities we have missed in making disciples for Jesus because we failed to witness to mercy and to potential disciples of Jesus simply because the people we encountered were vulnerable; they were nobody. Sometimes, we tend to forget our own past. We forget that like the blind man Bartimaeus, Jesus found us along the way when everyone else abandoned us; when we were nobody. Pope Francis says: "The master is calling you" (Mk 10:49). Not so that we can be special, not so that we can better than others, not so that we can be functionaries, but only because we are grateful witnesses to the mercy which changed us" (105).

The kind of joy Bartimaeus experienced is the joy that flowed from Jesus' witness to mercy. Mercy, indeed, restores human dignity. What really changed about Bartimaeus after encountering Jesus? Did he become rich? Perhaps no. He did not ask Jesus for money. He asked for one thing "that he may see." Often times we meet such people in our daily exercise of ministry and we think that they are a bother. In fact, all they need from us is sometimes just a word of encouragement, a ministry of presence and their story will change for the better. Poverty, vulnerability, susceptibility and the like robs people of dignity. Like Pope Francis once said, we must begin to smell like the sheep. In a homily the Holy Father delivered on Holy Thursday, 2013, he said the following: "...This I ask you: be shepherds, with "the odor of the sheep," make it real, as shepherds among your flock, fishers of men" (10). He says again, "We need to "go out," then, in order to experience our own anointing, its power and its redemptive efficacy: to the outskirts" where there is suffering, bloodshed, blindness that longs for sight, and prisoners in thrall to many evil masters" (9). The beginning of our down fall as priests and dispensers of God's mercy is when we neglect the flock entrusted to us. Jesus in whose priestly ministry we share has stated without any ambiguity that he came not for the healthy but for the sick. Until, we truly become shepherds to those on the margins of society, our ministry will only be unto ourselves, for our self-edification instead of for the glory of God. The result is that we become often unhappy and dissatisfied because we have failed the very core of our mandate. Pope Francis says again:

> ...A fine image of this "being for" others can be found in the Psalm 133: "It is like the precious oil upon the head, running down upon the beard of Aaron, running down upon the collar of his robe"(v.2). The image of spreading oil, flowing down from the beard of Aaron, upon the collar of his sacred robe, is an image of the priestly anointing, which through Christ, the Anointed One, reaches the ends of the earth, represented by the robe (7).

From the above quote of the Holy Father, it is clear our priestly anointing is for the edification of those entrusted to our care. Our priestly joys do flow from the exercise of this responsibility in season and out of season. Our woes also flow from the fact that we fail to dispense these graces given us on account of the flock entrusted to us. Pope Francis goes on to bring out the rich symbolisms inherent even in the robes or garments the priests put on for the celebration of the Sacraments. He says:

> The sacred robes of the High Priest are rich in symbolism. One such symbol is that the names of the children of Israel were engraved on the onyx stones mounted on the shoulder pieces of the ephod, the ancestor of our present-day chasuble: six on the stone of the right shoulder piece and six on that of the left (Ex. 28:6-14). The names of the twelve tribes of Israel were also engraved on the breastplate (Ex. 28:21). This means that the priest celebrates by carrying on his shoulders the people entrusted to his care and bearing their names written in his heart. When we put on our simple chasuble, it might well make us feel, upon our shoulder and in our hearts, the burdens and the faces of our faithful people, our saints and martyrs who are numerous in these times (8).

He added that:

> From the beauty of all these liturgical things, which is not so much about trappings and fine fabrics than about the glory of our God resplendent in his people, alive and strengthened, we turn now to a consideration of activity, action. The precious oil which anoints the head of Aaron does more than simply lend fragrance to his person; it overflows down to 'the edges." The Lord will say this clearly: his anointing is meant for the poor, prisoners and the sick, for those who are sorrowing and alone. My dear brothers, the ointment is not intended just to make us

> fragrant, much less to be kept in a jar, for then it would become rancid... and the heart bitter (8).

We are ordained for the people not for ourselves. Thus our ministry will be fruitful if and only if we were available to the flock. The Letter to the Hebrews says:

> Every high priest is taken from among men and made their representative before God, to offer gifts and sacrifices for sins. He is able to deal patiently with the ignorant and erring, for he himself is beset by weakness and so , for this reason, must make sin offerings for himself as well as for the people. No one takes this honor upon himself but only when called by God, just as Aaron was. In the same way, it was not Christ who glorified himself in becoming high priest, but rather the one who said to him...(Hebrews 5:1-5).

We must be humbled to accept our own place in God's plan for humanity. Our duty is first of all, to accept the invitation to ministry and allow God's grace to aid us point God to a fallen humanity.

CHAPTER FOUR

THE NAME OF GOD IS MERCY

Jesus' way of witnessing is worthy of emulation. He always creates a friendly environment for dialogue. The story of Jesus encounter with the Samaritan woman at the well in John 4 is one of such friendly dialogues. He did not allow the Samaritan woman's question "How is it that you a Jew ask a drink of me, a woman of Samaria" to deter or discourage him (John 4:9)? This question seems insulting and could have annoyed Jesus to leave. But Jesus was patient because he wanted to give the woman life.

When Jesus assured the woman that the water he will give her was living water so that she does not need to come to draw water at the well again, her desire for novelty made her ask for that water. She said "Sir give me this water so that I may never be thirsty or have to keep coming here to draw water" (John 4:15). From every indication, she did not know what she was asking for. The seed of the Word fell on shallow soil and the shoots that sprang up had no root (Matthew 13:20-21). She had made progress but she still had a long way to go, so Jesus patiently dealt with her.

Jesus proved to us that the only way to prepare the soil of the heart for the seed is to plow it up with conviction. That is why Jesus told her "Go call your husband and come back" (John 4:16). Jesus as it were forced her to admit her sin.

Indeed, there cannot be conversion without conviction. There must first be conviction and repentance and then there can be saving faith. Jesus had aroused her mind and stirred her emotions but he also had to touch her conscience and that meant dealing with her sin.

Having been convicted of sin, the Samaritan woman began to witness to Christ. She went to the village and told the whole town that she had seen the Messiah. She said "Come and see a man who told me everything I have ever done. He cannot be the Messiah, can he? They left the city and were on their way to him" (John 4: 29-30). Thank God she at least heard about the fact that the Messiah will come and perhaps that was the living water she has been longing for.

As part of our witnessing as a Church, we are called to break the barriers of division, injustice and discrimination in our offices, schools, hospitals, market centers, even in our Church. It is only when we respect and treat each other as dignified persons created in the image and likeness of Christ, can our witnessing be fruitful. We are like fishermen who cast their net into the sea not knowing the type of fish they will catch. The public sinner is a potential witness of Christ like that Samaritan woman did.

St. Paul justifies why Jesus will break all social and religious barriers and enter into Samaria in search of a lost soul (the Samaritan woman). St. Paul says "But God prove his love for us in that while we were still sinners Christ died for us" (Romans 5:8). This is our hope as Christians. God fulfilled this promise to humanity by becoming man. Thus, the Word of God is true when it says "Hope deferred makes the heart sick, but a desire fulfilled is a tree of life" (Proverbs 13:12). So we can all appreciate the fact that at the heart of the Samaritan woman was a seed of immortality; a longing for a day of salvation. Are you in a seemingly hopeless situation? Are you a public sinner? Like the Samaritan woman, it is you Christ wants to use to witness to our generation. There is no hopeless situation at all. This is because we have Jesus, the source of living water, the living water that does not run dry. This woman did not come to faith in Christ immediately. Jesus was patient with her and in this, he sets a good example for us in our personal work and above all in the work of evangelization. Certainly, she was the least likely prospect for salvation, yet God used her to win almost an entire village because he showed her mercy.

FOUR LESSONS ON DIVINE MERCY DRAWN FROM THE SAMARITAN WOMAN AT THE WELL

On June 07, 2016, Bishop Robert Barron, Auxiliary Bishop of the Archdiocese of Los Angeles, addressed the English- speaking priests from around the world in Rome for the special Jubilee Celebration as part of the Year of Mercy. In his address, Bishop Barron, reflected on the Divine Mercy. He intimated that he met fathers from the Ghana, United States, Canada, Australia, Latvia, Cameroon, Ireland, Nigeria, and many other countries. Below is the summary of what he said:

> During the communion at the Mass which followed my talk, I saw hundreds of priests in their albs coming to the altar to receive the Lord, and I thought of the passage from the book of Revelation concerning the white-robed army gathered around the throne of the Lamb.

As a basis of his presentation, Bishop Barron used the wonderful story from the fourth chapter of John's Gospel concerning Jesus' conversation with the woman at the well.

From this encounter, he derived four principles regarding the Divine Mercy. First, he asserts that God's mercy is **relentless**. Customarily, pious Jews of the first century would have assiduously avoided Samaria, a nation, in their minds, of apostates and half-breeds. Yet Jesus, journeying from Judea in the south to Galilee in the north, moves right through Samaria. Moreover, he speaks to a woman in public (something that men simply didn't do) and he consult with someone known to be a sinner. In all of this, Jesus embodies the love of God, which crosses barriers, mocks taboos, and overcomes all of the boundaries that we set for it. Thomas Merton spoke of the Promethean problem in religion, by which he meant the stubborn assumption that God is a distant rival, jealous and protective of his prerogatives. In point of fact, the true God is filled with *hesed* (tender mercy) and delights in lifting up human beings: "The glory of God is a human being fully alive."

And this conduces neatly to his second point, namely, that the divine mercy is **divinizing.** At times, we have the impression that God's mercy serves a reparative or healing purpose alone, that it solely binds up the wounds of our sin and suffering. That God's love heals is obviously true, but this tells but part of the story. Jesus asks the woman at the well for a drink, thereby inviting her to generosity. When she balks, citing the customary taboos, Jesus says, "If you knew who was asking you for a drink, you would have asked him, and he would give you living water." This, Bishop Baron told the priests in Rome, is a pithy expression of the central principle of spiritual physics, what St. John Paul II called "the law of the gift." As St. Augustine knew, we are all wired for God, hungry for absolute reality. But God, as St. John knew, *is love*. Therefore, to be filled with God is to be filled with love, which is to say, self-emptying. The moment we receive something of the divine grace, we should make of it a gift and then we will receive more of the divine grace. In a word, our being will increase in the measure that we give it away. This is the "water welling up to eternal life" that Jesus speaks of. God wants not merely to bind up our wounds; he wants to marry us, to make us "partakers of the divine nature."

The third principle Bishop Barron identified is that the divine mercy is **demanding.** He told the fathers gathered in Rome that we tend to understand the proclamation of the divine mercy according to a zero-sum logic, whereby the more we say about mercy, the less we should say about moral demand, and vice versa. But this is repugnant to the peculiar both/and logic of the Christian gospel. As Chesterton saw so clearly, the Church loves "red and white and has always had a healthy hatred of pink!" It likes both colors strongly expressed side by side, and it has an abhorrence of compromises and half-way measures. Thus, you can't overstate the power of the divine mercy, and you can't overstate the demand that it makes upon us. Jesus tells the woman that she comes daily to the well and gets thirsty again, but that he wants to give her the water that will permanently quench her thirst. St. Augustine accordingly saw the well as expressive of concupiscent or errant desire, the manner in which we seek to satisfy the deepest hunger of the heart with creaturely goods, with wealth and power, pleasure and honor. But such a strategy leads only to frustration and addiction and hence must be challenged. Indeed, Jesus shows that the woman exhibits this obsessive, addictive quality of desire in regard to her relationships: when she says that she has no husband, Jesus bluntly states, "yes, you've had five, and the one you have now is not your husband." This is not the voice of a wishy-washy relativist, and anything-goes peddler of pseudo-mercy and cheap grace. Rather, it is the commanding voice of one who knows that extreme mercy awakens extreme demand.

Finally, the divine mercy, bishop told the priests, is a **summons to mission.** As soon as she realizes who Jesus is and what he means, the woman puts down the water jar and goes into town to proclaim the Lord. The jar symbolizes the rhythm of concupiscent desire, her daily return to worldly goods in a vain attempt to assuage her spiritual hunger. How wonderful that, having met the source of living water, she is able to set aside her addictions and to become, herself, a vehicle of healing for others. The very best definition of evangelization that the bishop intimated is: "one starving person telling another starving person where to find bread." We will be ineffective in our evangelizing work if we simply talk, however correctly, about Jesus in the abstract. Our words of proclamation will catch fire precisely in the measure that we have been liberated and transformed by Christ.

Bishop Barron concluded by asking all who read these words to pray for the priests who gathered in Rome that week? "Beg the Lord that we might all become bearers of the divine mercy," he said.

In reflecting deeply on the four principles of Divine Mercy that Bishop Barron outlined, I find them very true. First, that God's mercy is **relentless c**annot be over-emphasized: grace comes first- gracias prima. In his pursuit of us God is relentless. The Samaritan woman comes to the well alone at the hottest part of the day and there was Jesus. God is relentless in his search for us in season and out of season, in the face of social and gender stereotypes (because according to Jewish custom Jesus cannot have anything to do with a Samaritan because the Jews considered them impure race and worse of all she is a woman; an adulterer) which society places on us. **Catholic Hymn Numbered 317 sums up the relentless nature if God**. Again, in the parable of the lost sheep, Jesus demonstrates the relentless nature of God in pursuit of his wayward children:

> The Tax Collectors and sinners were all drawing near to listen to him, but the Pharisees and Scribes began to complain saying, "This man welcomes sinners and eats with them." So to them he addressed this parable. "What man among you having a hundred sheep and losing one of them would not leave the ninety-nine in the desert and go after the lost one until he finds it? And when he does finds it, he sets it on his shoulders with great joy and upon his arrival home, he calls together his friends and neighbors and says to them, "Rejoice with me because I have found my lost sheep.' I tell you, in just the same way there will be more joy in heaven over one sinner who repents than over ninety-nine righteous people who have no need of repentance (Luke 15:1-7).

The parable of the Lost Sheep defies logic. The shepherd takes 100 sheep to pasture, one gets lost, the shepherd leaves the 99 sheep in the wilderness and went in search of the one lost sheep. What if the shepherd comes back to find the ninety-nine sheep scattered and lost? This is absurd. The absurdity that this story entails is the very message Jesus communicates to us. It is the sheep that gives the shepherd the most problem and yet it suffices to say that this is the one who deserves careful and greatest attention. The Good Shepherd find the lost sheep and puts it on his shoulders instead of spanking it. This is perhaps the reason why on the Solemnity of the Sacred Heart, the gospel reading reflects the story of the Good Shepherd. Mercy is one of the greatest attribute of the Good Shepherd for the one who shows mercy is also a Good Shepherd. We are invited to imitate the Good Shepherd by holding out our hearts to others (showing mercy) instead of scolding them in their moments of vulnerability. This is what Bishop Baron intimates when he says: **God's mercy is relentless.** Relentless because he never gives up on us. He is always out there in search of his wayward children. This is what Estelle White communicates to us in her song "Oh, the love of my Lord is the essence."[2]

Oh, the love of my Lord is the essence
Of all that I love here on earth.
All the beauty I see he has given to me
And his giving is gentle as silence.

Every day, every hour, every moment
Have been blessed by the strength of his love.
At the turn of each tide
He is there at my side,
And his touch is as gentle as silence.

There've been times when I've turned from his presence,
And I've walked other paths, other ways.
But I've called on his name in the dark of my shame,
And his mercy was gentle as silence.

Second, **God's mercy is divinizing**. The Samaritan woman had to submit to divine grace; the source of living water. When we encounter God's mercy, it divinizes us; it transforms us with its divine grace. The work of divinizing is always God's unfailing initiative. Man, divinized, has been the original plan of God. in Psalm 8, the Psalmist says:

O Lord our Lord, how awesome is your name through

---

[2] Estelle White (C) McCrimmon Publishing Co Ltd, Great Wakering, Essex, England.

all the earth!

I will sing your majesty above the heavens with the mouths of babes and infants.

You have established a bulwark against your foes, to silence enemy and avenger.

When I see your heavens, the work of your fingers, the moon and the stars that you set in place- what is man that you are mindful of him and a son of man that you care for him?

Yet you have made him little less than a god, crowned him with glory and honor.

You have given him rule over the works of your hands, put all things at his feet: All sheep and oxen, even the beasts of the field, the birds of the air, the fish of the sea, and whatever swims the paths of the seas.

O Lord, our Lord,

How awesome is your name through all the earth.

God divinized man at creation, and the Psalmist agrees when he says: "Yet, you have made him little less than a god, crowned him with glory and honor. You have given him rule over the works of your hands, put all things at his feet" (Psalm 8:6-7). Ephesians 1 augments the divinization of man when it says:

> ...Blessed *be* the God and Father of our Lord Jesus Christ, who has blessed us with every spiritual blessing in the heavenly *places* in Christ, just as He chose us in Him before the foundation of the world, that we would be holy and blameless before Him. In love He predestined us to adoption as sons through Jesus Christ to Himself, according to the kind intention of His will, to the praise of the glory of His grace, which He freely bestowed on us in the Beloved. In Him we have redemption through His

blood, the forgiveness of our trespasses, according to the riches of His grace which He lavished on us. In all wisdom and insight He made known to us the mystery of His will, according to His kind intention which He purposed in Him with a view to an administration suitable to the fullness of the times, *that is,* the summing up of all things in Christ, things in the heavens and things on the earth. In Him also we have obtained an inheritance, having been predestined according to His purpose who works all things after the counsel of His will, to the end that we who were the first to hope in Christ would be to the praise of His glory. In Him, you also, after listening to the message of truth, the gospel of your salvation-having also believed, you were sealed in Him with the Holy Spirit of promise, who is given as a pledge of our inheritance, with a view to the redemption of *God's own* possession, to the praise of His glory. (Ephesians 1:1-14)

Third, **Divine Mercy is demanding; a vibrant paradox**. God's mercy does not come to him who does not make any effort. Grace perfects nature. The Parable of the Merciful Father in Luke 15 is a practical example. Mercy demanded that the lost son comes back to his senses and when he came back to his senses, mercy found him. The vibrant paradox lies in the fact that the young man had to go through all those unfortunate moments (tending swine, longing to feed on the pods of the swine) before coming back to his senses. Mercy presupposes remorsefulness on the part of the penitent. Sometimes, I think God allows our weaknesses to confront us so that he can humble us, for we often become too complacent.

Fourth, **Divine mercy is a summons to mission**. This finds concrete expression in Jesus's command to the

Samaritan woman to "put down the water jar." Jesus summons the Samaritan woman to put down the water jar, and that act of putting down the water jar symbolizes her putting down her sinful past. Unless we heed to Jesus's summon to put down our various water jars (our most cherished sins that give us short term pleasures), there cannot be conversion. Unless we are changed by Jesus, we cannot evangelize; we cannot go on mission. Evangelization is simply making the love of God known and cherished and so the one who communicates this love must of necessity experience this love himself or herself. It is only the one who has truly experienced Jesus who can go talk about him like the Samaritan woman did. The highest life of the Church is a life of mission. That is why the Mass, the highest prayer of the Church cannot end without ITE MISSA EST (Without being sent on mission). That is why we do not spend long hours in Church. The mission field is ripe; the real missionary job is out there. I have always told my parishioners that in Church, we are all angels, but it is out there that our Christian life is tried and tested. If dressing beautifully and coming to Church like we do every Sunday is what Christianity is all about, then Christianity is very cheap indeed.

The above four principles Bishop Barron puts stress on as regards the Divine Mercy give a new dimension and twist to our appreciation of the Divine Mercy.

CHAPTER FIVE

JESUS COMES TO US WHEN WE RECOGNIZE THAT WE ARE SINNERS

> He then addressed this parable to those who were convinced of their own righteousness and despised everyone else. "Two people went up to the temple area to pray; one was a Pharisee and the other was a tax collector. The Pharisee took up his position and spoke this prayer to himself, ' O God, I thank you that I am not like the rest of humanity—greedy, dishonest, adulterous—or even like this tax collector. I fast twice a week, and I pay tithes on my whole income.' But the tax collector stood off at a distance and would not even raise his eyes to heaven but beat his breast and prayed, 'O God, be merciful to me a sinner.' I tell you, the latter went home justified, not the former; for everyone who exalts himself will be humbled, and the one who humbles himself will be exalted." (Luke 18:91-14)

There are two dangerous sins that no human being should dare commit: Self-righteousness and Presumption. In his book *The Name of God is Mercy,* Pope Francis says: "The first and only step required to experience mercy is to acknowledge that we are in need of mercy. Jesus comes for us, when we recognize that we are sinners" (x). The Holy

Father further explained that those who are in the habit of judging people from above, who are sure of their own righteousness, who are used to considering themselves just, good, and in the right, do not feel the need to be embraced and forgiven. These people fall within the category of self-righteousness. And there also are those who feel the need but think they are irredeemable because they have done too many bad things, and they fall within the category of the sin of presumption.

No matter how terrible we think our sins are, Jesus wants to hear them because he never gets tired of listening to nasty stories and forgiving us. Like the story of the woman caught in adultery, Jesus always tells the sinner "...neither do I condemn you. Go and sin no more." All the Lord requires of us is to admit our faults and experience his mercy and love anew. Alone with Jesus after her accusers had left, the story of the woman caught in adultery teaches and reminds us that in the confessional, the sinner is alone with a merciful God; a God who promises that "When we confess our sins, he is faithful and just to forgive us and to cleanse us from all unrighteousness" (1 John 1:9). In the event of God's forgiving you, your accusers will be nowhere to be found. In fact, they do not matter in this encounter at all. In the sight of the Lord, they stand condemned, and so they will leave one by one. The interesting thing is that the Holy Father intimated that "the woman did not claim to be a victim of "false accusation," she did not defend herself by saying, "I didn't commit adultery." No, "she acknowledged her sin" and answered Jesus by saying, "No one condemned me Lord." And so, Jesus said, neither do I condemn you. Go (and) from now on do not sin anymore." Therefore, Francis concluded, "Jesus forgives. But here there is something more than forgiveness. Because as confessor, Jesus goes beyond the law." In fact, "the law stated that she must be punished."

What is more, Jesus "was pure and could have himself cast the first stone." But Christ "goes further than that. He does not say adultery is not a sin, but he does not condemn her with the law." This is "the mystery of the mercy of Jesus" (xv).

It is in the very nature of God to forgive. God may seem to tarry in inflicting punishment on us. According to St. Thomas Aquinas, it is not a sign of weakness that God is merciful, rather than a sign of weakness, it is the mark of his omnipotence. The psalmist says:

> Out of the depths I call to you, Lord;
> Lord, hear my cry!
> May your ears be attentive to my cry for mercy.
> If you, Lord, keep account of sins, Lord, who can stand?
> But with you is forgiveness and so you are revered... (Psalm 130:1-4).
>
> In other words, the psalmist reminds us that we revere God above all because he forgives. This is indeed a sign of his omnipotence.

There is nothing more interesting and fascinating about people than to know that each one of us has a weakness. No matter our unique personalities, we are all weak in some measure. What brings about weaknesses and strengths lie in our temperament, which is what Tim Lahaye in his book *Spirit-Controlled Temperament* has asserted:

> It is temperament that provides each human being with the distinguishing qualities that make each as individually unique as the differing designs God has given to snowflakes. Temperament is the unseen force underlying human action, a force that can destroy a

normal and productive human being unless it is disciplined and directed. Temperaments provides both our strengths and weaknesses. Although we like to think only of our strengths, everyone has weaknesses. God has given Christians the Holy Spirit, who is able to improve our natural strengths and overcome our weaknesses- as we cooperate with him... (v)

From the above, Tim establishes the fact every human being is beset with weaknesses and at the same time has strengths. However, human beings always focus on weaknesses at the detriment of strengths, and so many have resigned to self-pity. So many people are hurting and wounded because people have made them feel so; they have been labeled and they have accepted these labels and are wondering if ever they possess some strengths. This is where the ministry of mercy becomes paramount. This book offers hope for all who because of their weaknesses have become depressed and resigned to despair. Ministry of mercy brings out the strength in you and makes you see God as greater than your weakness. Ministry is people-centered. Therefore, anything that will restore the dignity of the human person is what ministry is about. We must all work toward educating all Christians about the fact that ministry is a vocation; a vocation that calls on all the baptized to sacrifice for the growth of the body of Christ, the Church.

The psalmist says in Psalm 139:

You formed my inmost being;
You knit me in my mother's womb
I praise you, because I am wonderfully made
Wonderful are your works

The vision of God for man is found in this. Man, in spite

of his weaknesses, is fearfully and wonderfully made. God looks beyond the weakness of man and focuses rather on the strength that man possesses. In the Parable of the Merciful Father (Prodigal Son), we are told that:

> ...while he was still a long way off, his father caught sight of him and was filled with compassion. He ran to his son, embraced him and kissed him. His son said to him, "Father, I have sinned against heaven and against you; I no longer deserve to be called your son" but his father ordered his servants, 'quickly bring the finest robe and put it on him; put the ring on his finger and sandals on his feet. Take the fattened calf and slaughter it. Then let us celebrate with a feast, because this son of mine was dead and has come to life again; he was lost and has been found.' Then the celebration began (Luke 15:20-24).

The heart of confession is not the sins we declare, but the divine love we receive. God is not interested in what we have come to confess. Instead, he delights in conveying to us his divine life which we have lost through sin. In other words, he does not focus on our weaknesses but targets our strength which is his divine life in us to strengthen us. This should give every Christian hope. If one examines the words of the Merciful Father critically, one cannot but be moved by the urgency with which the father communicates divine life to his son. Let us examine these words together.

First, "...while he was still a long way off, his father caught sight of him and was filled with compassion" (v.20a). This presupposes that the merciful father has been waiting for the return of his wayward son. He knew he will come back one day a destitute. Perhaps, the merciful father will always go out there expecting to see his destitute son return; perhaps it was a daily routine for he caught sight of him and had compassion on him. The merciful father did not go out there with a frowned face to castigate his wayward son. He goes out there compassionate and patiently expectant that his son will come back.

Secondly, “He ran to his son, embraced him and kissed him” (v.20b). Can you imagine the Father, an old man running to meet his destitute son? Showing mercy makes us youthful. In order to convey his divine life to us, because of its urgency, God runs to meet us. He embraces us, and he kisses us. This is a sign of true love: agape, self-sacrificing, unconditional love.

Thirdly, the young man’s confession and the reaction of the merciful father deserve our commendation: “’Father, I have sinned against heaven and against you; I no longer deserve to be called your son’ but his father ordered his servants, ‘quickly bring the finest robe and put it on him; put the ring on his finger and sandals on his feet. Take the fattened calf and slaughter it” (v.21-23). The attitude of the ‘son’ as expressed in his words was a sign of remorse and admission of faults which every repentant sinner must have. But worthy of note is the ‘father’s’ response to his repentant son. The ‘father’s’ attention was on the servants at that moment when his son was confessing his sins commanding them to reinstate his destitute son. God’s divine mercy is the basis of his divine justice. His fore-giving act which enables him to forgive us even before we confess our sins is a clear indication that his desire to communicate love to us supersedes everything else.

Finally, there was a celebration; an expression of God’s joy. And what is the celebration about? That a destitute and a wretched son has come back after having wasted his father’s property in **dissolute** living. Such a celebration should be for a responsible son not a wayward one. God is joyful when he forgives us; when he communicates divine life to his sinful children. God's heart as represented in the Sacred Heart of Jesus is a human heart, too, a heart that goes out to his wayward and destitute children. We are told that the father of the prodigal son saw him from afar as he approached his father's house and had compassion on him. The word 'compassion' is from the Hebrew root word 'racham' which means 'womb.' Therefore, having the heart of a mother, the father's heart goes out to his prodigal son. Which mother does not suffer with her child even when the child deserves that suffering?

Reflecting on the intense joy of the Merciful Father in having his son back safe and sound, Pope Francis has this to say in his *With the Smell of the Sheep: The Pope Speaks to Priests, Bishops, and Other Shepherds*:

> In contemplating with awe this superabundance of the Father's joy that is freely and joyously expressed when his son returns, we should not be fearful of exaggerating our gratitude. Our attitude should be that of the poor leper who, seeing himself healed, leaves his nine friends who go off to do what Jesus ordered, and goes back to kneel at the feet of the Lord, glorifying and thanking God aloud. Mercy restores everything; it restores dignity to each person (p. 27).

We ought to be grateful to God and rejoice with those who have been shown mercy. The Holy Father adds: "This is why effusive gratitude is the proper response: we have to go party, to put on our best clothes, to cast off the rancor of the elder brother, to rejoice and give thanks..."(p. 28). What kind of heart is God having such that having been hurt by us he (God) rejoices when he shows us mercy.

In the same vein, when we are faced with weaknesses, we must be bold to face them. According to Tim Lahaye in

Spirit-Controlled Temperament,

> A good rule of thumb is this: when you determine your temperament on the basis of your strengths, don't change your mind when we get to your weaknesses. That may indicate a reluctance to be objective or honest with yourself. Strengths carry corresponding weaknesses, so face them realistically, then let God do something to change them (p. 68).

It is said that a habit formed at childhood becomes a tyrant at old age. One cannot form a habit over many years and expect to change overnight. It is not magic. To unlearn those habits, it may also take some time. Prayer is key, but it does not take away weaknesses overnight. Prayer mitigates daily the effects of our weaknesses such that these weaknesses do not overwhelm us. Some people come to confession complaining of committing the same sins over and over again. Sometimes, they wish to sleep and wake up one day and all their weaknesses are gone. It does not work that way. It needs patience, endurance as St. Paul intimated in Romans 5:1-5,

> Therefore, since we have been justified by faith, we have peace with God through our Lord Jesus Christ, through whom we have gained access by faith to this grace in which we stand and we boast in hope of the glory of God. Not only that but we even boast of our afflictions knowing that affliction produces endurance, proven character, and proven character, hope and hope does not disappoint, because the love of God has been poured out into our hearts through the Holy Spirit that has been given to us.

The strength we acquire through prayer is to contnue

hoping. One must begin to focus on one's strength because every weakness comes with a corresponding strength. Whenever we only focus on our weaknesses, we magnify our weaknesses and make them bigger than God. God whose name is mercy is bigger or greater than all our weaknesses and problems. Aside prayer giving you hope, it gives you joy. This joy comes from the Holy Spirit again who assists you in prayer. According to Tim Lahaye,

> The second temperament characteristic of the Spirit-filled person is joy. In his commentary on St. Paul's letter to the Galatians, R.C.H Lenski, a great Lutheran theologian, gave this comment concerning the gracious emotion of joy:
>
> > Yes, joy is one of the cardinal Christian virtues; it deserves a place next to love. Pessimism is a grave fault. This is not fatuous joy such as the world accepts; it is the enduring joy that bubbles up from all the grace of God in our possession, from the blessedness that is ours, that is undimmed by tribulation (p. 89).

This means that the joy provided by the Holy Spirit is not limited by our circumstances or our daily struggles. Many think that one has to be joyful only when things are good. This illusion has led many people to question God when bad things happen to them even though they serve him. But they have confused happiness with joy. John Hunter once said, "Happiness is something that just happens because of the arrangement of circumstances, but joy endures in spite of circumstances." (90). God uses our weaknesses as attraction point to draw us to himself (cf. Evangeli Gaudium no. 6 and 7).

CHAPTER SIX

THE QUALITY OF MERCY

One of the greatest works of William Shakespeare, namely *MERCHANT OF VENICE*, captures succinctly the theme of mercy. This chapter analyzes each line within its wider context of human relations. Below is Portia's Speech at the Court Scene:

> The quality of mercy is not strain'd
> It droppeth as the gentle rain from heaven
> Upon the place beneath. It is twice bless'd;
> It blesseth him that gives, and he that takes.
> Tis mightiest in the mightiest; it becomes
> The throned monarch better than his crown:
> His scepter shows the force of temporal power,
> The attribute to awe and majesty,
> Wherein doth sit the dread and fear of kings;
> But mercy is above this sceptred sway,
> It is enthroned in the hearts of kings,
> It is an attribute to God himself,
> And earthly power doth then show likest God's
> When mercy seasons justice. Therefore, Jew,
> Though justice be thy plea, consider this-
> That in the course of justice none of us should see

salvation: we do pray for mercy,
And that same prayer doth teach us all to render
The deeds of mercy. I have spoke thus much,
To mitigate the justice of thy plea,
Which if thou follow, this strict court of Venice
Must needs give sentence 'gainst the merchant there"

(Act IV, Scene 1, MERCHANT OF VENICE)

The above speech was given at the Law Court by Portia during the trial of Antonio. The speech is regarded as one of the greatest speeches in Shakespeare's writings and is made by Portia, disguised as young lawyer Balthazar, who speaks with heightened eloquence to beg Shylock for mercy after traveling from the fictional town of Belmont to Venice. Mercy and forgiveness are enduring themes that pervade Shakespeare's works. The quote is an example of the esteem Shakespeare held for those who showed mercy as expressed in his poetry.

Shakespeare presented mercy as a quality most valuable to the most powerful, strongest and highest people in society. Professor Harold Fisch, formerly of Bar-Ilan University, has argued that the words of Deuteronomy 32:2, "My doctrine shall drop as the rain, my speech shall distil as the dew; as the small rain upon the tender grass, and as the showers upon the herb," were echoed in the first words of the speech, "The quality of mercy is not strained. It droppeth as the gentle rain from heaven upon the place beneath."

Portia explains with eloquence the value of human mercy to Shylock and why the virtue of mercy is very important. According to the speech, mercy is an important human virtue which transcends all worldly powers; it is also divine upon combination with human morality and justice. Through its representation of the Renaissance ethos, this poem puts up a plea for acquisition of liberal values and virtues.

According to Portia's speech, mercy is a form of compassionate treatment and is comparable to justice, which is applied by man as law. However, mercy is expected to be intrinsic and very natural and should never be forced. This makes it sincere in its application. The expectation, according to the poem, is for everyone to have mercy since this is the only way one can be like our God, our creator. While justice appears bound to the earthly system, it can condemn, unlike mercy.

From the speech, the speaker follows the 'standard approach' to ask for Shylock's mercy. In the process, she reveals her own skills by the use of methodical mind. This kind of speech and argument is based on a careful process of human reasoning and not emotion. If one, therefore, has mercy, then it will be possible to have godlike powers and status. In the speech, Shylock is deeply concerned with justice while Portia preaches the significance of mercy in human beings.

What is important is that, while Portia's speech is well-reasoned and measured, Portia's ideas nonetheless try to pronounce mercy as the major polarizing issue existing between Christianity and Judaism. For instance, she offers frequent references to what appears divine and appealing. Mercy among human beings emerges as the best virtue for Christians. While one may think that Portia in the speech is simply offering a form of appeal, in retrospect we observe that her speech ends up becoming an ultimatum. It becomes, consequently, the final chance through which Shylock can adequately save himself. If he does not do that, then Portia will have the chance to crush all his legal expectations and arguments. Thus Portia says:

> Though justice be thy plea, consider this-

That in the course of justice none of us
should see salvation: we do pray for mercy,
And that same prayer doth teach us all to
render
The deeds of mercy. I have spoke thus much,
To mitigate the justice of thy plea,
Which if thou follow, this strict court of
Venice
Must needs give sentence 'gainst the merchant there"
(Act IV, Scene 1)

Within all dimensions of life, this speech by Portia offers a keen analysis and comparison between justice and mercy. By so doing, Portia manages to prove to the reader why the virtue is very important in our world and the best way to govern human behavior. However, the speech stresses the need for individuals 'to be' or 'not to be' depending on the society they are in. To be on the safe side, having mercy is the best thing. Therefore, the quality of mercy is intrinsic, unrivaled, and very natural.

Mercy is used to represent the New Testament, or Christianity, while justice signifies the Old Testament or Judaism. According to Christians, mercy is the only decisive approach towards attainment of natural justice. With mercy, one forgives and loves even all his or her enemies. This is therefore used as one of the best ways to present Godly love on earth. Generally, this speech by Portia is significant because it can be learned by many and also be applied in different situations confronting humanity today. By use of appropriate literary tools and poetic devices, this work remains one of the greatest works from the Shakespearean age.

Another important thing is the use of poetic devices in the speech. The first notable poetic device used in this speech is a *simile*. She says: "It droppeth as the gentle rain from heaven." Portia compares mercy with rain in the second line to show that mercy falls gently from the heavens, and the same way mercy should flow. Another literary approach used in the speech is *repetition* of same sound in the same line known as *alliteration*. In the poem, *alliteration* occurs in line ten, 'sceptred sway'. Another significant poetic device in the poem is the use of *syllable*. The syllables used here include *Too*, *The*, *Qua-li-ty*, and *Out*. Another common device here is *foot*. This consists of short or long syllables which make up what is called the *'metre'* within a particular poetic line. A good example of a foot in this poem is 'The Qua-li-ty of *mer/-cy'* is not strained. Such kind of foot in poetry is known as *'iambic'*. The use of metre as a major poetic device is present in Portia's poem. A metre usually consists of 'beats' or feet. In the line The Qua-li-ty of mer/-cy' is not strained we have five feet in what we have 'in iambus'. The poem is a complete unrhymed verse and is presented as in 'iambic' pentameter. Another form of poetic device employed is the use of allusions. In this poem, there is the use of biblical allusions to offer greater meaning of the intended message. In the thirteenth line, the poet says that 'mercy' is a strong power on earth that is comparable or equivalent to God's ability and might. Portia says: "It is an attribute to God himself."

"The quality of mercy is not strain'd"

In analyzing the above the line above, Shakespeare brings his readers to appreciate the fact that mercy is something that has to be freely given; no one can force someone else to be merciful. The word "Strain'd is an old form of the word "Constrained" which means forced. It straineth not to be merciful, but overall makes one richer in character. It costs one nothing to forgive, except one's own pettiness. To forgive is not petty, nor is it to be brushed aside as a casual thing, but it is ultimately of great importance.

It droppeth as the gentle rain from heaven

The 'gentle rain' metaphor demonstrates this: the bible says (as Shakespeare well knew) that 'God sends the rain to fall on the just and the unjust.' It is not that God is ultimately not in a position to pass judgment, but that he is merciful, frequently giving better than we deserve and is quick to forgive those that truly seek the same with bowed heart.

Jesus' admonishes us that "[i]f therefore you bring your gift to the altar but there recall that your brother has something against you, leave there your gift before the altar, and go first to be reconciled with your brother, and then come offer your gift (Matthew 5:23-24). "A true Christian believes that a man's relationship with God is predicated absolutely on his relationship with other men, and that God does not honor the prayer of a man who has not yet resolved his differences with others, as Christ Himself said: "And when you stand praying, forgive, if you harbor anything against another, so that, in turn, your Father in Heaven may forgive you your transgressions" (353-354) (Mark 11:25). Jesus continues, "For if you forgive others their transgressions, your heavenly Father too will forgive you; if, however, you do not forgive others, neither will your Father forgive your transgressions (Matthew 6:14-15). This is the essence of Christ's teaching, the very foundation of true Christian beliefs, which Jesus poignantly summarized. Ironically, in view of the history of Christian practice–Jesus directs those who would be his followers to heed well the words of the Jewish Prophet Hosea: "go and learn what this means: 'I desire mercy not sacrifice' (Matthew 9:13; cf.,

Hosea 6:6).

Instead of invoking the Lord's Prayer, Portia might have easily referred Shylock to the understanding of mercy expressed in the Torah and throughout the rest of Jewish Scripture as well. Specifically, for example, she might have cited a passage of crucial relevance to the Jewish perception of mercy, such as that found in the Book of Exodus (34:6-7): "The Lord passed before him (Moses) and proclaimed: The LORD! The LORD! a God compassionate and gracious, slow to anger, abounding in kindness and faithfulness, extending kindness to the thousandth generation, forgiving iniquity, transgression, and sin..."

The thronéd monarch better than his crown

This line builds upon the theme that Portia has set in motion; after all, who is mightier in the temporal world than the monarch? And, if indeed mercy is "mightiest in the mightiest" as she says, then it follows that mercy should be most abundant in those with the most power to grant it. At the same time, it makes the somewhat daring implication (for those who possess "Divine Right of Kings"), that it may not be the crown that makes the king. But what makes a king is the fact that he is kind and merciful.

His sceptre shows the force of temporal power

Here's another arguable fact; if you scan "temporal" as two syllables (TEMP-rul) rather than three, the line easily becomes pentameter with a feminine ending, which is probably closer to what Shakespeare intended given the usual contempt for 12-syllable lines in English poetry. **Sceptre** is a rod or small staff that is one of the three primary symbols of English royalty (the crown, the sceptre, and the orb being the regal trinity). **Force** in this context means "validity or legality" (given the presence of the word "power" in the same line). **Temporal** means "pertaining to this life or this world, not spiritual, not eternal; earthly" in this context (deriving from Anglo-French via the Latin *temporalis*, "of time"). Thus, Portia reminds Shylock that a king's power is ephemeral. God who is merciful is the only one who possesses power eternally and permanently.

The attribute to awe and majesty,

Other than the ending foot being a pyrrhic, there's nothing rhythmically noteworthy about the line. **Attribute** denotes "an object of close association; a symbol" and refers to the sceptre mentioned above. Portia is basically setting up a juxtaposition of those qualities of power that alternately inspire dread and reverence, a theme most famously explored by Machiavelli, who posited the question "whether it be better to be loved than feared or feared than loved?" Since this isn't the Machiavelli Resource Center, however, you can learn more about Machiavelli's thoughts on the matter by reading *The Prince*, Chapter XVII.

Wherein doth sit the dread and fear of kings;

Because this is the termination of a two-line dependent clause, this is one of those stretches in which the casual reader of Shakespeare can occasionally get confused. The line qualifies "awe and majesty" of the previous line; the two lines together describe the symbolism of the sceptre.

But mercy is above this sceptred sway;

And now, Portia shifts from the earthly to the ethereal. Just as God reigns above the king in the natural order, mercy is a more ennobling quality than the austerity of power represented by the sceptre. **Sway** means "rule or dominion."

It is enthronéd in the hearts of kings,

It's a matter of interpretation whether or not to inflect the "is" to make the first foot an iamb instead of a pyrrhic. However, the presence of all those short "i" vowel sounds versus the long "o" of "enthronéd" tends to make the spoken line sound that way no matter how you scan it. Note the choice of the word **enthronéd**, by the way, to reinforce the regality of mercy in a ruler.

It is an attribute to God himself;

Rhythmically, this line mirrors its predecessor, and, like the preceding line, the pyrrhic helps deliver emphasis to **attribute**. Portia's speech again employs a bit of anaphora to help the phrasing and rhythm set up for the next two lines. Effectively, Portia is reminding Shylock that even God, who wields the infinite capacity for revenge, is defined by His mercy. The name of God is mercy.

And earthly power doth then show likest God's

This line employs a masculine ending (an extra stressed syllable at the end of the line) as a variant, bringing more emphasis to the name of God at the end of the line. In her usage of **likest**, Portia is saying that earthly power is showing *most* like God's (as opposed to merely being similar). It's an interesting double comparison between mercy and justice, God and king.

When mercy seasons justice. Therefore, Jew,

From this point on, note how Portia keeps hammering at the words "justice" and "mercy" to make her point. **Seasons** (from the Middle English *sesounen*, deriving from the Anglo-French *seisoné*, meaning "brought to a desired state") is used in its archaic sense "to temper; to soften." Here's an interesting bit of trivia, by the way, since Portia is invoking God in this speech. The word "mercy" has 276 occurrences in the King James Bible, according to concordances; the word "justice" occurs 28 times. Ironically, the two have only one line in common: Psalm 89, verse 14 ("*Justice* and judgment are the habitation of thy throne: *mercy* and truth shall go before thy face"). And now, back to our regularly scheduled analysis....

Though justice be thy plea, consider this,

Iambic pentameter doesn't get much more straightforward than this. This line makes the turning point in Portia's speech (begun in the line above by "Therefore, Jew"). Up until now, she has been waxing philosophical on the topic of mercy. One might imagine Portia's delivery of the first 14 lines playing to the general audience within the court. Now she directly addresses Shylock in more practical and calculated terms regarding justice.

That, in the course of justice, none of us

The last foot scans best as a pyrrhic to place the proper emphasis on "none". Again, Portia is repeating the word "justice"—three times in successive lines—with much the same conscious effect that Marc Antony uses the word "honorable" in his funeral oration of *Julius Caesar*. In both cases, the speakers mean for their respective audiences to ponder the word and how it applies to the situation at hand. In Portia's oratory, she is attempting to get Shylock to be less rigid in his demand for justice. Ironically, she gives him the proverbial rope with which to hang himself in this speech because Shylock's eventual fate hinges on the strictest possible interpretation of the law.

Should see salvation: we do pray for mercy;

Rhythmically, the line is basic iambic pentameter with the now familiar feminine ending. **Salvation** (from Middle English *salvacion* via Anglo-French from Latin *salvation*, which derives from *salvare*, literally "to save") and **pray** are chosen carefully to bring home the following point: even the ultimate judge doesn't apply unadulterated justice. Portia is saying that is what we are counting on when we pray for God's mercy.

And that same prayer doth teach us all to render

Note how the pyrrhic/spondee combination at the beginning of the line helps emphasize the phrase "same prayer." This is a bit of foreshadowing that builds on the Duke's question to Shylock earlier in the scene, ""How shalt thou hope for mercy, rendering none?" In turn, the whole theme of the scene takes its cue from the Sermon on the Mount; to quote the King James Bible, Matthew 5:7, "Blessed are the merciful: for they shall obtain mercy." There are a number of New Testament quotations that echo the sentiment—James 2:13, "For he shall have judgment without mercy, that hath shewed no mercy; and mercy rejoiceth against judgment," comes to mind—and it is no accident that New Testament scripture forms the basis of Portia's rhetoric, aimed as it is at Shylock, a Jew. **Render** (from the Middle English *rendren* via Anglo-French deriving from the Latin *reddere*, meaning "to give back") means "to offer or grant."

The deeds of mercy. I have spoke thus much

It's a matter of preference in this line whether the third foot, split by the period, scans as an iamb or a pyrrhic. Whether one views it as a restatement of the Golden Rule, or karma, or whatever creed one pleases, Portia is essentially saying that as we pray for mercy for ourselves, so should we practice mercy upon others. Again, this can be seen as foreshadowing once one knows how the scene will end.

To mitigate the justice of thy plea;

Portia ends her speech by putting her motive out in the open (a sound rhetorical strategy for persuasive oratory, given that one of the primary aims of rhetoric is to cultivate credibility) and by returning to that familiar refrain of justice. **Mitigate**, meaning "to make less severe," comes to us from Middle English *mitigaten* via the Latin *mitigare* (pp *mitigatus*), meaning "to soften." It reinforces the symbiosis between justice and mercy.

Which if thou follow, this strict court of Venice

The pyrrhic/spondee scansion gives the proper dual emphasis on "strict court"; the feminine ending is probably due to the necessity of ending the line with "Venice" more than anything else. Portia is also deflecting any responsibility for Antonio's well-being from the court—after all, the court can only make their judgment based upon the law and the will of the plaintiff—and placing it squarely upon Shylock.

Must needs give sentence 'gainst the merchant there.

Portia extends an olive branch; Shylock will have none of it and so wreaks his own downfall out of stubborn pride. Is it justified? Shylock could have relented on numerous occasions during the scene. His refusal combined with a to-the-letter interpretation of his bond is what destroys him. It seems that Portia and the court is willing to meet even the vestige of mercy in kind. Yet, is humiliation a mercy? It is an ending easier to understand than it is to condone.

The attitude of Shylock in the court scene is a clear example of how unforgiving we are to one another. God has shown us so much mercy that he expects us to show each other mercy. Like Portia, God reminds us that mercy is His (God's) attribute and having been created in his image and likeness of God we ought to be merciful. In fact, God provides the grace to enable us forgive one another. When we fail to forgive one another, it will get to a time that God cannot show us mercy anymore. Here justice takes over, and that is why Portia passed the sentence on Shylock.

CHAPTER SEVEN

LIGHTENING THE LOAD

"Captives cannot free themselves," so goes the saying; they need someone to see them as captives who need releasing rather than as enemies to reject. "Father forgive them, for they know not what they are doing" (cf. Luke 23:24) was one of Jesus' last wish to his father as he hanged upon the cross. Did his captors not know what they were doing? They knew it. This was indeed a practical example that Jesus left for us his followers, yet forgiveness is one of the greatest challenges to our Christian life. How can we lighten the load of unforgiveness in our life? This chapter lays bare some pragmatic steps one can take in order to forgive to fulfill Jesus's vision for us to forgive one another unconditionally in the light of our exercise of ministry. This will be looked at in the following areas: recognition, resolution, renunciation, covering, and rebuilding.

1. RECOGNITION

Before one can begin the process of forgiveness, one must recognize one's hurt and name it for what it is. Sometimes, it is easy to deceive ourselves and pretend that we are not angry, but these experiences are ephemeral. Some experiences like hostility, resentment, and vindictiveness must bring about desire for a treatment before they can be treated. These experiences need to be brought to the master physician, Jesus Christ, who specializes in freeing captives—both the potential forgiver and the one needing forgiveness. If the problem is not rectified, its adverse effects can probably not be brought under control. This is a universal reality. The following questions can help us in our quest to recognize our need to forgive.

- Exactly what are you talking about?
- What feelings have been churning deep within you?
- When are you most likely to feel angry?
- What inhibitions has it brought to your life?
- Are there certain types of people who naturally raise hostility in you and what does that mean?

2. RESOLUTION

Secondly, the ability to resolve to forgive after identifying the pain is also very important. This is where inner conditioning to be a forgiving person is important. Forgiveness is a process. Sometimes the decision to forgive is taken, but after that the anger or pain resurfaces. This is where our will to forgive must surpass our emotions. The yardstick of our choice to forgive is Christ who forgave us while we were still sinners (Romans 5:8). Often the pain that resurfaces seems as if the incident happened yesterday when it actually happened long earlier. This is captivity; it is bondage. Friends, the resolve to forgive is out of obedience to God. This is the unavoidable starting point. Perhaps that is what Jesus was accomplishing on the Cross in the midst of his suffering—resolving to forgive his betrayers, and captors, no matter what. Often the will of God for our lives seems unpleasant but obedience to God leads to victory for us just as Jesus was victorious.

3. RENUNCIATION

Furthermore, forgiveness is an act of renouncing the desire to inflict similar pain on the offender. In fact, the instinct to return cruelty for cruelty dwells deep within us because the inner most parts of our lives can be very dark and mysterious places where evil can be hatched. This renunciation comes or requires a spiritual work, determination, and often an hour-by-hour choice. At other times, we are motivated by the action of Christ on the cross "Father forgive them, for they do not know what they are doing" (Luke 23:32). This is a stunning lesson. Is it not strange to see Jesus forgiving his captors? Thus, Christ invites us to protect the interests of our offenders just as he did on the cross.

4. COVERING

Forgiveness involves as well covering the sins of those we claim to be our enemies. The encounter between David and Saul when the latter decided to kill the former is a practical example. Even when Saul had been killed, David mourned for him in the following words:

> O Israel, your pride and joy lies dead upon the hills; mighty nerves have fallen. Do not tell the Philistine lest, they rejoice. How much they were loved, how wonderful they were both Saul and Jonathan (2 Samuel 1:19-20, 22-23).

If it were you or me, we would perhaps expose the weaknesses of those we claim to be our enemies, but David rather covered it by praising Saul. We can also learn a lesson from the relationship King David had with his rebellious son Absalom. Jonny Rashid's thought on "What we can learn from David and Absalom" cannot be over-emphasized. He intimated in his blog circleofhope.net that

> Some of the stories in the Old Testament are so practical and filled with wisdom that is so applicable, even in our modern era. My thought is that if we ask God to reveal himself in the stories, we'll see a lot more in the stories. Though we may lean toward deconstruction, I hope we end with application.

Reading 2 Samuel 13- 18, Rashid discovered some very important points for our consideration. The story of David and his son Absalom is an example of how unconditionally God loves us. When David heard of the death of Absalom who was trying to take his (David's) throne, he was in anguish and languished thus: "And the King was deeply moved and went up to the chamber over the gate and wept. And as he went, he said, "O my son Absalom, my son, my son Absalom! Would I had died instead of you, O Absalom, my son, my son (2 Samuel 18:33 ESV). One finds another type of this heart in the Old Testament. Let us examine the love of Jacob for Joseph. The story of Jacob's love for Joseph is a typology of the Sacred Heart of Jesus, a love that is compassionate and goes out in search of the lost. For instance, when Reuben brought words to Jacob about the death of Joseph, this is what Jacob said:

> **33** ..."It is my son's robe! Some ferocious animal has devoured him. Joseph has surely been torn to pieces."
> **34** Then Jacob tore his clothes, put on sackcloth and mourned for his son many days. **35** All his sons and

daughters came to comfort him, but he refused to be comforted. "No," he said, "I will continue to mourn until I join my son in the grave." So his father wept for him.

5. REBUILDING

Finally, the fifth step in the process of shedding the needless weight of resentment and anger is rebuilding. This means that whenever possible the forgiver invests strong energies in not only covering the wrong but also forgiving himself in loving ways to help the offender rebuild his or her life. When there is deep remorse for a wrongdoing, a person will live with the sorrow of it forever, a spiritual limp, if you please. Our job as people of the cross is to help lessen the limp. The story of Joseph in the book of Genesis (Genesis 45) is an epitome of rebuilding. In fact, in Joseph, all five of the steps I have enumerated can be found, namely recognition–where he saw what his brothers did to him as a blessing in disguise; resolution–resolving to forgive his brothers no matter what; renunciation–refusing to take vengeance when he had the opportunity to do it; covering–when he never blamed them for what they did to him. Indeed, he rebuilds that life between them from Israel to Egypt to overcome the famine.

In conclusion, it is very difficult to forgive, but the process I have discussed above: recognition, resolution, renunciation, covering, and rebuilding can be a recipe to forgiveness. Remember always that when we encounter someone who has offended us greatly in one way or another, we need to see that person as a spiritual captive not as an enemy. No matter how distasteful one's actions may seem to be, you must visualize the person as a captive and not your enemy. The enemy of God loves to take people's wills, passions, and actions captive. Do not be enslaved by hatred and unforgiveness because the power to forgive is in your hands. Will you act now?

To make my explanation on forgiveness more dramatic, I will focus on a story that illustrates the need for us to forgive one another without counting the cost. This story was culled from the *Priestly Echo* (a magazine/journal of the Archdiocese of Accra on which I served as editor) entitled "Lessons from the Past," written by Pascaline Songsore and reprinted here with permission:

~

Lizzy opened her eyes slowly. Her eyelids felt like a heavy load had been placed on them. She could faintly hear voices around her. She shut her eyes firmly and made another attempt to open them, this time a little more slowly than the first time.

"Doctor, she is opening her eyes," a voice very close to her exclaimed in excitement.

She had heard that voice before but could not immediately tell who it belonged to. She tried to speak and ask questions but her voice did not accompany her slightly open mouth.

"Hi, Madam Lizzy, this is Dr. Awotwe. Give my hand a squeeze if you can hear me."

It was then that she realized someone was holding her hand. Like an obedient child she gave the Doctor's hand a little squeeze.

"Great!" The Doctor said.

"The anesthesia is now wearing off, so we expect her to be like this for a while. She is doing well, no need to worry."

'Hospital?' Lizzy, thought. What could she possibly be doing here? The more she tried to find answers to the questions in her mind, the more she felt her head ache terribly. She drifted off into a deep sleep.

"She is still asleep." came a voice much later. Lizzy opened her eyes once again and this time with less difficulty.

"Mama, thank God you are up." An excited voice said.

"Where am I?" Estelle asked faintly.

"In hospital, mama. A car hit you this morning on your way to work."

Then she remembered. She left home that morning, very frustrated as her car had refused to start. In exasperation, she stood at the junction to her house, looking for a taxi that would take her to her office as fast as possible. She was scheduled to meet some investors who had expressed interest in the company she worked for. Her Chief Executive had fixed the important meeting for 8:00 a.m. but had asked her to come in thirty minutes earlier so they could go through their presentation. Lizzy's husband had left home much earlier since he had to drop off their last daughter at school before going to work.

As she searched through her bag for her cell phone to call Bob her mechanic, she did not see an oncoming car. She could only remember being hit hard, being lifted of the ground, falling to the ground, the excruciating pain that ran through her nerves, voices screaming, and then she passed out.

"Are you ok, mama?" Asibi, Lizzy's daughter asked.

This brought her mind back to the hospital. Before she could answer, the door swung open and in walked the doctor who had performed her surgery, accompanied by a nurse.

"There you are. Very wide awake. How are you feeling?" asked the Doctor while examining her.

"I.... I.... think I am okay. What was the surgery for?" Lizzy asked.

The doctor responded, "You had a hip fracture and we had to operate on it to correct it as soon as possible. It will take some time to heal, but you are doing well so far. We thank God the car did not run over you."

There was something familiar about the Doctor's voice and mannerisms that Lizzy could not identify. She looked like someone she had met before, but she could not immediately tell where. She seemed a very pleasant young woman.

Over the next few days, Lizzy recovered well. She received so much love and care from the young female doctor and wondered if that is how much attention she paid to all her patients. She would check up on her early in the morning, at lunch time and before she closed for the day.

Lizzy mustered courage a few days later and said, "Doctor, thank you very much for all your love and care. This has helped greatly in my recovery. I wanted to know more about you. You look very familiar. You look like someone I have met before, but I cannot tell where we met."

Dr. Awotwe smiled in her usual sweet manner and said.

"Madam Lizzy, there is nothing special about me. God has been very good to me over the years. My story is a very interesting one. My parents died when I was very young. I therefore had to live with my auntie who was a trader. I was told my late father was our village catechist, so the parish opted to pay my school fees. My auntie was a very busy woman and used to travel from Wa to Kumasi to buy different kinds of goods for sale: clothing, utensils, cloth, etc. One day she informed me that a stranger wanted to take me to Accra to work as a house help and that they had decided to sponsor me through school."

She continued, "I left Wa with my new family, not knowing what to expect. I had heard many stories about Accra and at age 12, I did not know what to expect. My new family treated me very badly from the start. I was given very hard work to do, given little food and punished severely for every little mistake I made. There were days I could not go to school because I could not finish my cleaning or washing on time."

Dr. Awotwe paused. She turned to look at Lizzy, who had her head bent.

"One day, the man of the house announced that he had lost some money. I was falsely accused of taking that money. I was locked up in the storeroom of the kitchen for half of the day to make me confess to the crime. I did not understand why I should confess to something I did not do. I was beaten up and my fingers were burnt with a hot iron...."

"Stop!" Lizzy screamed. "We are really sorry" she said in tears. "My husband and I were ignorant at the time. Over the years we have not been able to forgive ourselves. We searched for you, just to apologize, but were unsuccessful at finding you."

At this point tears were rolling down Estelle's cheeks uncontrollably. There was no doubt that this was the 12-year-old house help they had treated badly over twenty years ago.

"When I ran out of the house that evening, with my burnt fingers, I wanted to kill myself. I had endured so much in my young life and did not want to live anymore. I got hit by a car and was rushed to the hospital. The driver who hit me never showed up to check up on me or pay my bills. I lied to everyone that I was homeless for fear of being taken back to the house of pain. Then I met Dr. Naah, the owner of this hospital. She took me in, cared for me and my life changed completely from that time onwards."

"Please, forgive us," Lizzy pleaded. "We truly regret our actions."

"I forgave you long ago, only it has been hard to forget that part of my life, especially when I look at this scar." The doctor said as she showed Lizzy the ugly scar on her right hand. "I had the opportunity of having plastic surgery but I insisted I wanted my hand to remain this way. Anytime I look at it, it reminds me of how far God has brought me. I recognized you the very day you were brought in here. I was not on duty but I opted to take care of you."

She rose up from the chair at Lizzy's bedside and said, "I have to go and attend to other patients. I will see you later."

As Dr. Awotwe walked out of the room, Lizzy wanted to say something. She opened her mouth but no words came out. She and her husband had over the years regretted the bad treatment they meted out to Dr. Awotwe. They had gone to confession about it and their Parish Priest had counseled them on ways to deal with the guilt. Seeing Dr. Awotwe, again had made her feel guilty all over again.

When her family visited her later that day, she narrated the entire discussion she had with the Doctor. Mr. Taabasung, Lizzy's husband, was heartbroken. At the same time, they were amazed that this same girl had willingly treated Lizzy even though she knew who she was.

When the nurse came in to administer her evening medication, Mr. Taabasung requested to meet Dr. Awotwe.

"I am sorry sir, Dr. Awotwe started her leave today." The nurse said. "She only came in this morning to see your wife before traveling outside the country."

Lizzy could not believe this. "How long will she be away?" She asked the nurse.

"About a month, Madam. A new doctor will be seeing you till you are discharged," the Nurse responded.

This had been a great lesson for the Taabasungs. The weeks that followed were very humbling for the family. They prayed fervently that Dr. Awotwe would forgive them completely when they met her on her return to the country. They had visited her foster mother Dr. Naah, who had promised to assist them reconcile with her. They also volunteered to share the experience with other families in their Parish on how they should treat househelps and children who were not their own, but under their care.

So, my question now is: if you were Dr. Awotwe and the Taabasungs finally came to meet you and asked for forgiveness, what would be your response?

To err is human but to forgive is divine. I would like to conclude this story reiterating that unforgiveness is like a load. It takes captive of our wills. We need to lighten this load. I left the story hanging because both Dr. Awotwe and the Taabasung's represent a humanity struggling to forgive and be forgiven. This story is, therefore, meant for those who have been wronged and those who perpetuate wrong doing.

CHAPTER EIGHT

MARY MOTHER OF MERCY

In this journey of experiencing God's mercy, the Church presents to us a model of faith; a model of mercy, Mary the Mother of God. In the Salve Regina (Hail Holy Queen), the prayer begins:

Hail Holy Queen
Mother of Mercy
Hail our lives, our sweetness and our hope
To Thee do we cry poor banish children of Eve
To thee do we send up our sighs
Mourning and weeping in this vale of tears
Turn then most gracious advocate
Your eyes of mercy towards us
And after this our exile show onto us the blessed fruit of thy womb Jesus
O Clement, O Loving, O Sweet Virgin Mary

The Church has always been regarded as a mother. So, in Mary, we have a perfect and a concrete expression of what the motherhood of the Church is all about. If Jesus is the Divine Mercy, his blessed mother, Mary, is the Mother of Mercy. In *Misericordiae Vultus*, Pope Francis says of Mary:

> My thoughts now turn to the Mother of Mercy. May the sweetness of her countenance watch over us in this Holy Year, so that all of us may rediscover the joy of God's tenderness. No one has penetrated the profound mystery of the incarnation like Mary. Her entire life was patterned after the presence of mercy made flesh. The Mother of the Crucified and Risen One has entered the sanctuary of divine mercy because she participated intimately in the mystery of His love (24).

Mary understood the mission of her son more than anyone else. She embraced it even when she was warned by the prophet Simeon at the presentation of Jesus in the temple: "...Simeon blessed them and said to Mary his mother, 'Behold, this child is destined for the fall and rise of many in Israel and to be a sign that will be contradicted (you yourself a sword will pierce) so that the thoughts of many hearts may be revealed." (Luke 2:33-35). Mary from the very onset understood her role in our salvation plan and she played it to the end. First, Mary bore the Divine Mercy (Jesus) in her womb that propelled and summoned her for mission of service and evangelization to her cousin Elizabeth. We are told that Mary went in haste to the hill country of Judea and what ensued between her and Elizabeth was what will unfold later in the life of Mary and her son Jesus. In *Misericordiae Vultus*, Pope Francis says:

> Chosen to be the Mother of the Son of God, Mary from the outset was prepared by the love of God to be the *Ark of the Covenant* between God and man. She treasured divine mercy in her heart in perfect harmony with her Son Jesus. Her hymn of praise, sung at the threshold of the home of Elizabeth was dedicated to the mercy of God which extends from "generation to generation" (Lk 1:50).

> We too were included in those prophetic words of the Virgin Mary. This will be a source of comfort and strength to us as we cross the threshold of the Holy Year to experience the fruits of divine mercy. (*MV*, 24)

In the prophetic voice of Mary as regards God's mercy, Mary reminds us that God's mercy endures forever as captured by the psalmist in Psalm 136: "Praise the Lord, for he is good; for his mercy endures forever; Praise the God of gods; for his mercy endures forever; Praise the Lord of Lords; for his mercy endures forever" (v.1-3).

The Catechism of the Catholic Church describes Mary's hymn of praise (Magnificat) as "the song both of the Mother of God and of the Church" (CCC2619). I will add that in that same song, Mary reminds us of the divine mercy, above all, which is eternal. What a powerful witness to God's Mercy our blessed Mother demonstrated? Thus, she is also the Mother of Mercy. The Catechism of the Catholic Church captures beautifully:

> Mary's prayer is revealed to us at the dawning of the fullness of time. Before the incarnation of the Son of God and before the outpouring of the Holy Spirit, her prayer cooperates in a unique way with the father's plan of loving kindness: at the Annunciation, for Christ's conception, at Pentecost, for the formation of the Church, His Body. In the faith of His humble handmaid the Gift of God found the acceptance He had awaited from the beginning of time. She whom the Almighty made "full of grace" responds by offering her whole being: "Behold I am the handmaid of the Lord; let it be done to me according to thy word." "Fiat": this is Christian prayer: to be wholly God's because He is wholly ours. (CCC 2617)

Mary also witnessed and participated in the divine mercy when she closely followed her son to Calvary. Mary witnessed her suffering son who though innocent endured suffering because of the redemption of humanity. Mary witnessed her only son beaten, slapped, spat upon and innocently nailed to the cross. Mary also witnessed Jesus forgiving the 'good thief.' Pope Francis says:

> At the foot of the Cross, Mary together with John, the disciple of love, witnessed the words of forgiveness spoken by Jesus. This supreme expression of mercy towards those who crucified him show us the point to which the mercy of God can reach. Mary attests that the mercy of the Son of God knows no bound and extends to everyone, without exception. Let us address her in the words of the *Salve Regina,* a prayer ever ancient and ever new, so that she may never tire of turning her merciful eyes upon us and make us worthy to contemplate the face of mercy, her Son Jesus. (*MV*, 24)

I will add that Mary's experience of God's mercy reached its climax when the dead body of her Son was placed on her lap. What we call the Pieta (an Italian word meaning Pity or Compassion, a subject in Christian art depicting the Virgin Mary cradling the dead body of Jesus, most often found in sculpture and designed by famous Michelangelo). In the Pieta, we see a mother who has endured suffering together with her only Son communicated to us. A quick look at the image of the Pieta readily lends to the interpretation that Mary was sorrowing for the death of an only Son. But a critical look will reveal a mother interacting with her Son asking him to fulfill his promise to her (Mary) and humanity that he will rise again (Resurrection). It was a moment of assurance of better things to come; a moment of hope not despair; a time of fulfillment which Mary invites us all to embrace. Indeed, Mary's hope in her son's resurrection was rewarded with her own assumption which the Church has declared as a dogma.

Examining all these things that the blessed mother endured in the light of her son's Passion, Death, and Resurrection, I add my voice to that of Jim Caviezel, a Hollywood actor in Mel Gibson's *The Passion of the Christ* on his call on Pope Francis to proclaim Mary as the Co-Redemptrix. He made this appeal in Amsterdam during the 2019 World Day of Peace. Proclaimed as a Co-mediatrix is not just enough because by proclaiming Mary as a Co-Redemptrix, we affirm her participation in our redemption not only at the Annunciation but during the Paschal Mystery (Passion, Death, and Resurrection) of Jesus Christ. Jim Caviezel recalled St. Pope John Paul II's call on all Christians to be co-redeemers with Jesus and Mary. The more you experience the Passion of Christ, the more you understand the COMPASSION of blessed Mother, the connection between Mary and Jesus. He then asked this fundamental and thought-provoking question: "What mother does not suffer when her child suffers?" St. Teresa of Calcutta also exclaimed that Mary is the Co-Redemptrix with her Son because she gave Jesus her body that brought us salvation. When Jesus was arrested, it was only Mary who understood her unified mission with her son in our redemption. She was not seen fighting the soldiers who arrested her innocent Son or even uttered a word. During the Passion, Jesus meets his sorrowful mother and that moment Jesus experienced a new lease of life: the strength to continue his mission. At the foot of the Cross, when Jesus saw his Mother and John the beloved disciple, he gave his mother to John and indeed to all of us as our spiritual mother. Even Jesus acknowledges the co-redemptive role of his mother.

O Lord, our Lord, how awesome is your name through all the earth! Even as we thank God for the gift of Mother Mary to humanity, for through her obedience Christ was born for our salvation, we would like to reflect on what makes her the Mother of Mercy. In Luke 1:39-56, when Mary visited Elizabeth, the mother of John praised her for her unshakable faith in God which gave her the singular honor of becoming mother of the Savior. In response to the greetings and accolades Elizabeth showered on Mary, Mary burst out in a hymn—the Magnificat. In that Hymn, Mother Mary said: "The Mighty One has done great things for me, Holy is His name! From age to age His mercy extends to those who live in His presence" (vv.49 & 50). It is in this hymn that Mary, as Mother of Mercy, is revealed because she herself continually lived in the presence of the Lord. As such, the mercy of God was always upon her and made it possible for God to perform marvels in her life. According to St. Pope John Paul II in *Dives in Misericordia*: "Mary is...the one who obtained mercy in a particular and exceptional way, as no other person has" (9). The point is that those who experience the mercy of God should endeavor to be witnesses of mercy.

The month of May and October are traditionally months of the Holy Rosary. Here the Church invites us to pray every day with Mother Mary as we contemplate the mysteries of her Son's life, death, and resurrection. In praying the Rosary, Mary's role as Mother of Mercy is again made manifest. In the Hail Mary prayer, we pray: "...holy Mary mother of God, pray for us sinners, now and at the hour of our death."

The Apostle Paul says in Romans 3:23 that we have all sinned and have fallen short of the glory of God. Mary's role, then, from her place in Heaven is to pray for us who stand in need of God's mercy. She fulfils the role of Queen Esther (Esther 4:17), "never ceasing to pray" to her Son for the salvation of her people as they confidently fly to her for refuge in their trials and dangers. Therefore, each time we pray the Rosary, Mary's task as Mother of Mercy is accomplished because just as the pleading of Queen Esther won for the Jews mercy from King Ahasuerus, the prayer of Mary wins for us the mercy of her Son.

In a Marian hymn (CH 283) we pray, "O gentle, chaste, and spotless maid, we sinners make our prayers through you; remind your Son that He has paid the price of our iniquity. Virgin most pure, O star of the sea, pray for the sinner, pray for me." This stanza vividly illustrates the role of Mary Mother of Mercy in the life of the Christian who has recourse to her.

The Church celebrates the 7th of October as a memorial in honor of "Our Lady of the Rosary," recalling the victory at the battle of Lepanto. This is to emphasize the power in the weapon of the Holy Rosary. History has it that in praying the Rosary a physical battle was won. In this Extraordinary Jubilee of Mercy, we join our faith with that of the Mother of Mercy, believing that our spiritual battle against sin and evil will also be accomplished. Let us always remember that anyone who has experienced the mercy of God ought to be a witness to mercy. Before the conclusion of *Misericordiae Vultus*, Pope Francis dedicates one chapter to a reflection on "Mother of Mercy" praying that the sweetness of her countenance will watch over us in this Holy Year so that we may all rediscover the joy of God's tenderness. I add my voice to that of the Pope to encourage readers to be more fervent in seeking the maternal solicitude of Mary Mother of Mercy.

The words of *The Memorare* also affirm that Mary is the Mother of Mercy:

> Remember, O most gracious Virgin Mary, that never was it known that anyone who fled to thy protection, implored

thy help, or sought thine intercession was left unaided. Inspired by this confidence, I fly unto thee, O Virgin of virgins, my mother; to thee do I come, before thee I stand, sinful and sorrowful. O Mother of the Word Incarnate, despise not my petitions, but in thy mercy hear and answer me. Amen.

The words "before thee I stand, sinful and sorrowful" and "in thy mercy hear and answer me" are clear indications that Mary is the Mother of Mercy. *The Memorare* reflects the prayer of a child in need to his or her mother's compassion; it is a prayer of a sinful and remorseful child to a merciful mother. It is a reminder to our blessed Mother Mary that she who was full of grace at the very moment of her conception in the womb of Anne her mother and preserved from the stain of original sin through her Immaculate Conception cannot but be gracious. "...[T]hat never was it known that anyone who fled to thy protection, implored thy help or sought thine intercession was left unaided" shows how close our blessed mother is to her sinful children. Which mother does not suffer when her child suffers? It will be bizarre and absurd for our mother to abandon us at the very moment we need her most. There is no way the mother of mercy who bore Jesus, the face of the Father's mercy, ever abandons us. This confidence in her unfailing support makes the Church focus her gaze on her especially in troubled times. Mary exhibits the maternal nature of the Church. When we say the Church is a mother, it means that the Church finds concrete expression in the motherhood of Mary. Whatever qualities Mary exhibited during her earthly life both in joys and sorrows is what the Church truly exhibits. A Church that does not become a mother cannot be fruitful. The Holy Father writes in *With the Smell of the Sheep*:

> The Church--Benedict XVI told us—does not grow through proselytism, she grows through tenderness, her maternity, the witness that generates ever more and more children... the Church grows younger when she is capable of generating more children; she grows younger the more she becomes a mother. This is our mother, the Church and our love for children. To be in the Church is to be at home, with mom; at mom's house. This is the grandeur of revelation... (p. 180).

"Mary the Mediatrix of all Graces, pray for us who have recourse to thee" is part of the Catena Prayer legionaries pray during their meetings. In this short prayer, the Church acknowledges Mary as one who mediates the grace of God for her children. In answer to the question, "Why is Mary referred to as the Mediatrix?" Fr. William P. Saunders of Catholicstraightanswers.com permitted use of his response:

> The Second Vatican Council dedicated the eighth chapter of the *Dogmatic Constitution on the Church* to our Blessed Mother. Since our Lord continues His work and saving mission through His body, the Church, the council fathers, particularly under the guidance of Pope Paul VI, decided that it was most appropriate to address the role of our Blessed Mother in this document because "she is endowed with the high office and dignity of the Mother of the Son of God, and is ...the beloved daughter of the Father and the temple of the Holy Spirit" (#53). The whole Church honors Mary as a preeminent and wholly unique member of the Church, and as a model in faith, hope, and charity.
>
> Given this basis, the Vatican Council II here again repeated the titles of Mary as Advocate, Helper,

Benefactress, and Mediatrix (#62). In its basic definition, a mediator is one who serves as an intermediary between two other parties. Oftentimes, the mediator assists in reconciling differences and bringing the parties to an understanding.

Examining the references to our Blessed Mother in the Sacred Scriptures, we find this role of "mediator." Mary, recognized by Archangel Gabriel as full of grace, one with the Lord, and blessed among all women, conceived by the power of the Holy Spirit and bore Jesus Christ. Through her "mediation" Jesus entered this world– true God becoming also true man. In the gospel passages in which she appears, our Blessed Mother always presented our Lord to others: the shepherds, the Magi, the priest Simeon, and the wedding party at Cana. She stood at the foot of the cross, sharing in our Lord's sufferings, and at that point He gave her to us as our Mother. Finally, Mary was with the apostles at Pentecost; she who brought Jesus into this world was there for the birth of the Church. At the end of her life, Mary was assumed body and soul into heaven, the fulfilment of the promises of eternal life of body and soul given to all of the faithful. The *Dogmatic Constitution on the Church* captured her life well in stating, "Thus in a wholly singular way she cooperated by her obedience, faith, hope and burning charity in the work of the Savior in restoring supernatural life to souls" (#61).

Therefore, we could look at Mary as the Mediatrix in three senses:

- First, as mother of the redeemer, she was the intermediary through which the Son of God entered this world to save us from sin.

- Second, by the witness of her own faith and thereby of presenting Christ to others, she aided in reconciling sinners to her Son. Mary, sinless yet knowing the suffering caused by sin, continues to call sinners to her Son. Through her example, she inspires all of us to the faith, hope, and love that our Lord wants all of us to have.

- Finally, because of her assumption and role as mother for all of us, she prays for us, interceding on our behalf just as she did at Cana, asking the Lord to bestow graces to us as He wills.

This title and role of Mediatrix, however, in no way is meant to distract the faithful from Christ or erode His role as the one Mediator (#62). Christ's mediation is primary, self-sufficient, and absolutely necessary for our salvation, whereas the mediation of our Blessed Mother is secondary and dependent upon Christ. The Vatican Council stated, "In the words of the apostle [St. Paul], there is but one mediator: 'for there is but one God and one mediator of God and men, the man Christ Jesus, who gave Himself a redemption for all' (I Timothy 2:5-6). But Mary's function as mother of men in no way obscures or diminishes this unique mediation of Christ, but rather shows its power. But the Blessed Virgin's salutary influence on men originates not in any inner necessity but in the disposition of God. It flows forth from the superabundance of the merits of Christ, rests on His mediation, depends entirely on it, and draws of its power from it. It does not hinder in any way the immediate union of the faithful with Christ but on the contrary fosters it" (#60).

Let us continually implore our Blessed Mother's prayers. May her example inspire us to strive to be full of grace, seeking forgiveness for sin, and to present Christ to others in our words and deeds. As she held Christ in her womb, may we hold Christ in our hearts. In so doing, we too may become like mediators, leading others to Christ through our own witness.

CHAPTER NINE

MERCY IN THE LIGHT OF *MISERICORDIAE VULTUS*

It is appropriate that St. Pope John Paul II instituted Divine Mercy Sunday especially when we reflect on how Jesus responds to the apostles who had deserted him during his passion. Instead of rebuking Thomas or the rest of the apostles for their doubts and fears, the first words he speaks when he appears to them are "Peace be with you." Then he breathes the Holy Spirit on them. By the power of the Holy Spirit, he gives them a task: they are to be his official representatives in forgiving sins through the Sacrament of Reconciliation: "Whose sins you forgive, they are forgiven..."

What we see here is the great outpouring of Divine Mercy that flows from the wounded side of Jesus as presented in the Divine Mercy image given to us by St. Faustina. Let us take a look at someone who had a powerful insight into the Divine Mercy aside Sr. Faustina. Her name is Mother Angelica of blessed memory. I am sure most of us have heard of the Poor Clare Nun who founded the Eternal Word Television Network, EWTN. She tells a story in one of her live audiences about how she encountered the Divine Mercy at a beach in California. Even though she wore legs braces at the time, she liked to get close to the surf. A large wave came in and the water covered her shoes. Then she heard a voice,

'Angelica, that drop represents all your sins, all your imperfections and all your frailties. Throw it in the ocean.' She threw it back. Then she heard the Lord say, 'The ocean is My mercy. Now if you looked for that drop, would you ever find it?' 'No, Lord,' she replied. Mother Angelica then told the people in her audience that their sins are like that drop in the ocean. 'Every day, every minute of the day, throw your drop in the ocean of His mercy. Then, don't worry, just try harder.'

Every day we should throw our sins, all of our struggles, and sufferings into the ocean of Divine Mercy and make a fresh start just as St. Thomas did when he witnessed the wounds of Jesus. As we continue to reflect on the Divine Mercy, may we encounter Jesus in a deeper way, remembering that he gives us the ultimate act of Divine Mercy on the cross as blood and water poured from his side to cover our sins, to give his love and grace, to remove our doubts and fears of what lies ahead in our life's struggles in order to give us peace so we can say with St. Thomas, "My Lord and My God."

Praise be to our God who is Alpha—Beginning—and Omega—End (Rev 22:13), let us come boldly before the throne of grace where we will find mercy in time of need (Hebrews 4:16). This book, as a companion after the Year of Mercy, wishes to lead its esteemed readers to come to the consciousness of mercy as grace for beginning anew. In the Jubilee Year of Mercy, as the Church called on us to emphasize more on forgiveness and mercy than on the regrettable stance of punishment and excommunication, there is the need to understand the dynamics of mercy. Mercy is an opportunity for a new beginning. Whenever we have a genuine experience of God's mercy, we must bring ourselves to the point of beginning anew. We truly are given a fresh page to write our life's history. The Mercy of God is such that He does not recall our past transgressions (Is 43:25, Hebrews 8:12).

To begin anew requires setting praiseworthy goals and working with determination to attain those goals. There is a need to blot out any tendency of entertaining fears of failure due to past experiences. I have realized that there are so many Christians who, though they have encountered the Mercy of God, still sit in the ashes of guilt. Whenever a Christian does that, he or she refuses to grow physically, psychologically, spiritually, and emotionally. The prophet Isaiah says: "No need to recall the past. Can you not see that I am doing something new?" (Is 43:18-19). May this holy outpouring of God's mercy that has brought us to a new beginning give us courage in our struggle against sin.

The words of St. Augustine—"Let us commit our past to the mercy of God, our present to his faithfulness and our future to his providence"—give me hope. I think it should give hope to all. That is why the Church celebrates 40 days of Lent every year to enable us tie the loose ends of our lives and begin afresh. Lent is a time for a new beginning, a time when the Church celebrates mercy in a very definitive way. If Easter is the greatest feast of the Church, then the Lenten season, which is our preparation to celebrate this great feast, must lead us to appreciate God's gift of mercy and forgiveness. That is why on the eve of his passion, Jesus epitomized his saving love in the gesture of washing the apostle's feet. Washing another's feet was a gesture of a slave. People at most wore simple sandals, and on long journeys on dirt roads they collected lots of dust on dry days, mud on wet days, and animal waste always. That Jesus himself would take on the form of a slave and do this service for his disciples shows all of us that there was nothing he wouldn't do to serve us and save us.

Most people would feel very uncomfortable at that type of

service, at that type of love, but Jesus insisted on giving it. Only a few days before, when Jesus was dining in the house of Martha, Mary, and Lazarus, Mary anointed Jesus's feet with 300 days worth of priceless oil on Jesus—ten times what the 30 silver pieces Judas would receive for betraying Jesus—but Jesus defended her, saying she was doing it for his burial and that we wouldn't always have him (Cf. John 12:1-8). On another occasion when a woman washed his feet with her tears and dried them with her hair, Simon the Pharisee criticized Jesus for not recognizing the woman was a sinner. But Jesus said that she would be forgiven much because she had loved much and expressed that love for Jesus by that gesture of washing his feet, something that Simon himself did not do when Jesus entered his house because he did not love Jesus at all (Cf. Luke 7:36-50).

By his own action Jesus was "loving much" and showing how he was willing to "waste" not just a year's work but his whole life to wash our feet. We need to have faith to allow Jesus to love us in this extreme way. St. Peter, as we see, was very uncomfortable with this prospect. "You will never wash my feet," he exclaimed. But Jesus replied that unless he did so, Peter would have no part of him. In order to be part of Jesus, in order to enter into consecration, we need to allow him to clean us. Peter, realizing this and wanting to be totally for the Lord then gave him (Jesus) permission to wash his hands and head as well (Cf. John 13:1-17).

Jesus' gesture and dialogue with Peter gives us a chance to examine our own receptivity to what God wants to do in us. What does it mean for us to have our feet washed? The early saints of the Church, when they looked at Jesus' statement that once we have been washed only our feet need to cleansed, said that this is meant to refer to the sacraments of Baptism and Penance. In Baptism, we are thoroughly washed, but over the course of our journey each day, our feet come into contact with filth of the world and we need to allow Jesus to cleanse us. That is what he does in the Sacrament of Reconciliation, where Jesus is continually on his knees at our feet and not only carries out the service of a slave but dies to take away our sins. This is ministry at the service of mercy. We need to allow Jesus to clean not only the soles of our feet but our immortal souls. One of the reasons why Jesus performs this last rite at the beginning of the Last Supper is to show us that before he gives his body and blood, he wants and needs to cleanse us.

The season of Lent is a special time of grace for us Christian pilgrims to concentrate more on developing our spiritual lives. Traditionally, the Lenten culture is one of intensified prayer, fast and alms giving. This culture is fashioned to put us into the right frame of mind to reflect on the Pascal Mystery (Passion, Death, and Resurrection) of our Lord and Savior Jesus Christ. The season of Lent is therefore an opportunity for us to repent of sin, make reparation for sins committed and resolve to avoid the occasions of sin.

Lent begins with Ash Wednesday. On this day, a praxis known as the "imposition of ash" is observed in our church traditions. The ashes are prepared from burnt palm branches used during the previous year's Palm Sunday celebrations. The ash is then blessed and used to mark the foreheads of all pilgrims with the admonition "repent from your sins and be faithful to the Gospel" or with the reminder "you are dust and to dust you shall return." So, a sincere and conscious reception of ashes on Ash Wednesday is a sign that we admit our sinfulness and in a spirit of humility and repentance plead for clemency, God's forgiveness, and reconciliation. There cannot be true reconciliation without the admission of faults. This means that our readiness to embark on the discipline of Lent is always met with the mercy of God.

In *Misericordiae Vultus*, Pope Francis admonishes that

the season of Lent in this Jubilee Year be lived more intensely as a privileged moment to celebrate and experience God's mercy. The Pope recommends that in every diocese a "24 Hour Adoration of the Lord" be celebrated on the Friday and Saturday preceding the Fourth Week of Lent, emphasizing that we place the Sacrament of Reconciliation at the center in such a way that it will enable people to literally touch the grandeur of God's mercy with their own hands. God's mercy is extravagant, and that is what we celebrate during Lent. May every season of Lent be for us a moment to tap from the ocean of God's extravagant mercy.

Mercy gives us freedom from slavery to sin. Ghana's Independence Day is commemorated on the 6th of March. The independence of a nation signifies the end of colonial rule and the freedom given to a nation to govern herself. This means that even though we talk of the independence of a country, there still exists a system of governance. Osagyefo Dr. Kwame Nkrumah is quoted to have declared at the independence of Ghana that "Ghana our beloved country is free forever!" He added a thought provoking declaration in saying that "the independence of Ghana is meaningless without the total liberation of the African continent." This is profound in relation to what sin does to the sinner and to the entire human family and, conversely, to what freedom from sin does to the sinner and humanity in general.

In John's Gospel chapter 8, the message of freedom from the slavery to sin is made evident. At the end of the trial of the woman caught in adultery, Jesus asked whether no one remained to condemn her. After her response in the negative, Jesus then acquitted and discharged her saying: "I do not condemn you either. Go, but do not sin again" (John 8:11). In this same chapter, in a discourse with the Pharisees, Jesus without mincing words says, "I am telling you the truth: everyone who sins is a slave of sin" (John 8:34). This means that sin can be enslaving; it can be addictive. But then doing good can also be enslaving. It is therefore better to be a slave to that which is good and praiseworthy than to that which is evil and shameful. St. Paul puts it eloquently in Romans 6:18-20 when he says, "You were set free from sin and became the slaves of righteousness. At one time you surrendered yourselves entirely as slaves to impurity and wickedness for wicked purposes. In the same way you must now surrender yourselves entirely as slaves of righteousness for holy purposes."

In *Misericordiae Vultus*, the Pope affirms that "the Church's first truth is the love of Christ" and specifically mentions that "the Church [make] herself a servant of this love and [mediate] it to all people" (12). This, he says, is a love that forgives and expresses itself in the gift of oneself. In other words, the Church is a "slave" to communicating the mercy of God in order that wherever Christians meet, they should find an oasis of mercy. I wish to draw our hearts to the consciousness that the mercy of God gives us freedom from the slavery to sin and rather places us under the governance of righteousness. Mercy then becomes a source of joy for those who avail themselves for them.

The resurrection of Jesus on Easter Sunday is a clear sign that our time of slavery to sin is over. Mercy, therefore, is the source of Easter Joys. Perhaps, reflecting on the events before and after the resurrection of the Lord, St. Pope John Paul II, declared the second Sunday of Easter as Divine Mercy Sunday. In the *Misericordiae Vultus*, Pope Francis affirms that "God's justice is his mercy given to everyone as a grace that flows from the Death and Resurrection of Jesus Christ" (21). He emphasizes the point by saying that the Cross of Christ is God's judgment on all of us and on the whole world precisely because, through it, God offers us the certitude of love and new life. This is Divine Mercy. After forty (40) days of intensified prayer, fasting and alms giving in the Season of Lent, we now observe the joyful Season of Easter. The truth is that, we are joyful because His story did not end on the Cross. Death has been defeated, victory has been won! A New life that is glorious emerges.

Indeed, Mercy is our source of Easter Joys. We must remember that Mercy is Jesus himself. In essence, we are saying that Jesus himself is the source of our resurrection from the grave of sin. Jesus himself is the source of the new life that liberates. In the story about the prodigal son in the Gospel of Luke chapter 15, the prodigal son says "... I will arise ..." (Lk 15: 18). Here, to 'arise' is to resurrect. And it is the power of God that accomplishes resurrection. In Rom 8:11, St. Paul makes it clear that if the Spirit of him who raised Jesus from the dead is living in you, he who raised Christ from the dead will also give life to your mortal bodies because of his Spirit who lives in you.

Naturally we know that when we break a law, we sin. So, justice is called upon as a fundamental notion for any civil society that is governed by the rule of law. In this perspective on justice, emphasis is placed on the mere observance of the law that judges people and places a permanent label on them either as just or sinners. And when people are labeled as sinners, others who are not in that category are not to go close to them. Jesus who is the face of the Father's mercy defies that prescription and rather keeps company with those that the law considers sinners so that he can bring them to experience the resurrection. The message is that mercy is not opposed to justice but rather expresses God's way of reaching out to the sinner, giving him a new opportunity to look into himself, convert, and believe so he can be saved.

MERCY FOR WORKERS

In the highly capitalist economy that we find ourselves in today, an age of consumerism and materialism, we need mercy for Workers and Unemployed. Our beloved country Ghana also joins other nations to mark this day as "International Workers Day" or "May Day". In these celebrations, emphasis is placed on the dignity of work. In *Laborem Exercens* (an encyclical by St. Pope John Paul II on Human Work), we are reminded that our life is built up every day and derives its specific dignity from work. This document reiterates the fact that the Church is convinced that work is a fundamental dimension of our existence on earth (n.4 of Chapter 2). St. Paul also stated at a point that the apostles gave a rule to the people of Thessalonica that if a man will not work, he shall not eat (2 Thess 3:10). The point is that work makes us fully human and God in His mercy made us co-creators by mandating us to be fruitful and to multiply and, in addition to that, to fill the earth and subdue it (Gen 1:28). We can say that even though these words do not explicitly and directly refer to work, they, without a doubt, indirectly indicate resourcefulness which in itself implies work.

By Mercy for workers, this reflection seeks to draw attention to the puzzle of "just remuneration" for work done among other things. The point is that in designing the condition of workers, profit should not be considered over and above the principle of the common use of goods. In other words, every dignified work should provide a just remuneration for the work of an adult who is responsible for a family means providing remuneration that will suffice for establishing and properly maintaining a family and providing security for its future. But this usually is not the case. In our country, the average worker very often receives a wage that will not sustain him and his family. In the celebration of the Extraordinary Jubilee of Mercy, the Church calls on those who own and control the means of production, the decision makers in our country, and employers to reconsider the issue of just remuneration.

Furthermore, the issue of unemployment is on the ascendency. There are many people who have the requisite qualifications, who are willing to work but have no opportunity to work. In this unfortunate dilemma, we are required to be merciful with the unemployed. This is not a way of encouraging laziness but of seeing through the plight of the unemployed what the Father sees in the eyes of the sinner (compassion). This can be made practical if organizations and employers would make effective their policies and budgets for corporate social responsibility which finds expression in what the Church stipulates as corporal works of mercy (feed the hungry, give drink to the thirsty, shelter the homeless, visit the sick, visit prisoners, bury the dead, and give alms to the poor).

We are called upon to be Merciful like the Father (Luke 6:36). The theme chosen by the Holy Father, Pope Francis, to celebrate the Extraordinary Jubilee of Mercy is based on the words of Luke 6:36, "Be merciful just as your Father is merciful." The Pope describes this theme as "a programme of life which is demanding as it is rich with joy and peace" (*MV*, 13). He drew our attention to a few verses before the statement in Lk 3:36 where Jesus made it clear that His command is directed to anyone willing to listen to His voice (Lk 6:27). It means that "to be capable of mercy, therefore, we must first of all dispose ourselves to listen to the word of God...rediscovering the value of silence in order to meditate on the Word that comes to us" (*MV, 13)*.

It is becoming increasingly clear that our world has lost the value of contemplative silence. Our Liturgical gatherings are very often noisy, and there is so much noise in our neighborhoods and on our streets. The playing of loud music is a characteristic feature at most of our ceremonies. With all the noise around us we find it difficult to experience the value of silence. If we are to rediscover the value of silence, our priests should emphasize the silent periods within the Mass and draw the attention of the congregation to those silent periods. When we gather for communal prayers in our devotional groups and societies, we should implement periods of silence, and when we take time off to pray as individuals we should observe some silence in our prayer. By so doing, we will grasp more fully the message in the Word of God which essentially will lead us to be merciful like the Father.

In this pilgrim journey, each of us needs Mercy. The world we live in is not our home. Therefore, our sojourn through this world is a pilgrimage to Heaven. As sojourners, we need to remain aware that we are all constantly exposed to the devastation of sin that can hinder our attainment of our true goal (Heaven). But the good news is that out of God's gratuitous love, mercy is shown us on our pilgrimage. In *Misericordiae Vultus*, Pope Francis makes it clear that life itself is a pilgrimage and the human being is a visitor, a pilgrim traveling along the road, making his way to the desired destination. The point is that our desired destination as human beings (creatures) is to return to our Creator who dwells in Heaven. St. Augustine would say, "God you made us for yourself and our hearts are restless until they rest in you." It is this understanding of the human life as a pilgrimage that occasions the spiritual exercise of making a pilgrimage to the Holy Door in Rome or to a Holy Door in any other place in the world. The symbolism of a door is taken from Jesus' declaration in the Gospel of John 10:7, "Truly, I say to you, I am the gate (door) of the sheepfold."

The Holy Father says a pilgrimage to a Holy Door will be a sign that mercy is also a goal to reach and that it requires dedication and sacrifice. This means that every human being needs to make a pilgrimage to Jesus in order to embrace God's mercy.

In order to make strides on the journey of life, the pilgrim Christian should guard against judging and condemning others. He or she should work rather on forgiving others and giving to better the lives of others. It is when we have fulfilled all these conditions that we can say that we are being merciful like the Father. We ought to remember what God's word says right after it enjoins on the children of God to be merciful like the Father in Lk 6:37-38, "Do not judge others and you will not be judged; do not condemn and you will not be condemned; forgive and you will be forgiven. Give, and it will be given to you; a good measure, pressed down, shaken up and running over will be poured into your lap. For the measure you use for others will be the measure God will use for you." This, therefore, becomes the passport for our pilgrimage. The truth is that God comes to our assistance with His mercy every step of the journey. My prayer is that all who read this will embark upon their personal pilgrimage so as to serve as an impetus to conversion.

MERCY FOR MARRIED COUPLES

We need mercy as married couples. If there is any institution that is under a serious attack today, it is the marriage institution. The divorce rate is on an ascendancy. In his Apostolic Exhortation on the Family in the Modern World (*Familiaris Consortio*), St. Pope John Paul II writes,

> Living in such a world, under the pressures coming above all from the mass media, the faithful do not always

> remain immune from the obscuring of certain fundamental values, nor set themselves up as the critical conscience of family culture and as active agents in the building of an authentic family humanism. Among the more troubling signs of this phenomenon, the Synod Fathers stressed the following, in particular: the spread of divorce and of recourse to a new union, even on the part of the faithful; the acceptance of purely civil marriage in contradiction to the vocation of the baptized to "be married in the Lord", the celebration of the marriage sacrament without living faith, but for other motives; the rejection of the moral norms that guide and promote the human and Christian exercise of sexuality in marriage (7).

The influence of circumstances on the consciences of the faithful, therefore, requires the mercy of God. In the book of Genesis, God the Creator says: "it is not good for man to live alone. I will make a suitable companion to help him." So the basis for marriage is the compassion of God for the loneliness of man. In other words, God looked with mercy on the sorry state of man and decided to make a helper for man. Marriage, therefore, must be lived in the spirit of companionship and compassion.

The truth is that marriage is a dynamic path to personal development and fulfillment. Therefore, consenting parties to a marriage covenant must bear in mind the basis of the marriage covenant in order to establish a relationship of companionship and compassion. In our world today, the institution of marriage has been bedeviled with many misconceptions. So many people enter marriage with erroneous mind sets. Some parties of a marriage covenant in our era look on marriage as a social intervention against the economic instability we currently experience. Others see marriage as a prestige to attain while others perceive it as a legalization of sexual escapades. There are other erroneous reasons why people enter into the covenant of marriage. They have totally set aside the Creator's intention of compassion for the sorry state of man's helplessness in the face of loneliness. This has resulted in broken marriages and increasing cases of divorce.

Married couples should remember that God hates divorce (Malachi 2:16). Married couples should always remember that it was out of compassion that God instituted marriage so that in the atmosphere of compassion, they would treat one another with mercy, being merciful as the Father. The point is that if you are merciful as the Father, you will try not to offend your spouse to warrant a divorce suit. And if you learn to be merciful like the Father, you will forgive your spouse for offences committed against you in the covenant of marriage. And for the many who are traumatized by the unfortunate experience of broken marriages, may St. Helena intercede for you that you may forgive the past hurts in your marriage.

CHAPTER TEN

SOME PERSONAL EXPERIENCES OF THE MERCY OF GOD

I dedicate this chapter to some experiences people shared as regards their personal encounter with the mercy of God. Sometimes the best way to think about life is to reflect upon death. When I think about my life and how I have offended God, all the opportunities I have had to love that I have turned my back on, how little I have done with the gifts he has given me, I hope he is merciful. When I reflect upon all my mistakes and sins, my pride and arrogance, I hope he is merciful. In the end, each must fall at the feet of God and beg for mercy. In the end it all comes down to mercy. Let us now strive to show others the mercy we hope to receive. St. Augustine once said, "Let a man's life be praised in so far as he asks for pardon." With the Psalmist, I say, "Lord turn your face from my sins and blot out my transgressions." Yes, God should turn his face from our sins and blot out our transgressions because they are disgusting and burdensome. The above sums up the fact that no human sin, however serious can prevail over or limit mercy.

A life of Divine Mercy
Julie Carrick

When I wrote the song "Mercy," I was sitting in the Blessed Sacrament Adoration Chapel at St. Joan of Arc Catholic Church in Phoenix, AZ. I was having a full-blown pity party with Jesus. I needed to hear that my life would be just fine and that all the pain I was feeling would be taken away. What I heard was "Julie, I love you." (I wept.) Then I heard, "Things are going to get worse before they get better." (I was incredulous.) "Mercy" was written down from what I heard the Lord tell me next. It came as lyric and music flooding my mind, heart, and soul. (I wept again in gratitude.)

Things did get worse... In 2004 my oldest daughter, at the age of 20, was raped and became pregnant. My middle child, a daughter just months out of high decided to move out into an apartment with a friend from school. Within a couple of months her boyfriend moved in, and I was crushed. My husband found an old high school girlfriend from many years ago on the internet and within a few emails back and forth both decided to leave their families and begin a new life together.

Through Daily Mass, the Divine Mercy Chaplet and a 20-decade rosary every day I was able to survive. The grace and strength I received let me experience the suffering I was going through and allowed me to better understand how to offer my suffering within the context of the Divine Mercy of Jesus Christ. By better understanding His suffering and love for me I was able to not only survive, but thrive. In the midst of my pain, I grew deeper in love with Jesus. I found a deeper bond with His Immaculate Mother. Mercy flooded my life with grace as I had never known before.

The months passed. My first grandson was born

premature and spent a month in the neonatal intensive care unit at the Scottsdale hospital. Our daughter was filled with grace when she needed it most to choose his life and hear the call of her life to be his mother. When he came home, I felt a truly holy presence in our house. God's gift of life brought the first ray of hope into our family's brokenness. A month later, my husband had a wonderful 'visit' from our dear Mother Mary and was a changed man. The truth of his life was laid bare and he ended the relationship. Our Marriage Sacrament was blessed with Divine Mercy and was strengthened beyond my imagining. My husband left his job with the Department of Public Safety (AZ highway patrol) and joined the ministry full time.

A year passed. Our middle child came back to us emotionally and began the journey back to the Catholic faith. She is now living fully her Catholic faith.

A few years passed. In 2008, I was diagnosed with Lung Cancer. On Holy Thursday, I had the entire upper lobe of my right lung removed to remove the cancer. I was told 6 months to a year would pass before I would know if or what of my vocal ability would be restored. I came home from the hospital on Divine Mercy Sunday weekend. My entire vocal range was restored, plus 3 additional notes, on Corpus Christi!

The Divine Mercy of Jesus Christ is not having his suffering take away our suffering. It is pure gift to us as we realize the privilege and purpose as we offer our suffering together with His. We grow in grace as we live a life in His Divine Mercy.

Confession and Mercy
Rev. Fr. Emmanuel Salifu

Two biblical stories both of women seem to have caught

the attention of Pope Francis in writing his apostolic letter: the first is *"Misericordia et Misera"*—a phrase he took from Saint Augustine's reflection of the woman caught in adultery in John 8:1-11, and the second is the woman with a bad name in Luke 7:36-50.[3] The story of these women revealed to me during the Year of Mercy and even after an amazing grace both dispensed and received. Two women shamed and judged by society ironically become, according to the grace of God, models of sainthood—they show us what it means to be a saint. **A saint is not a sinless person but a sinful person in search of mercy.**

Quite a number of people seek healing in their lives, and if there is a sacrament so powerful as to experience divine healing, it is the sacrament of confession. I know this not only because I listen and dispense mercy in the name of Christ and by the power of the Holy Spirit but most importantly because I am a recipient and a beneficiary of such healing.

Often people have mentioned how they feel shy of confessing their sins before a priest wondering what the priest would think of them. Make no mistake; these women knew what it meant to be ashamed. They felt their guilt and they did not deny their guilt. Instead of allowing the shame to be an obstacle, it became an instrument which propelled them to experience mercy. The Latin word *"misericordia"* can be subdivided into two words *"miseria"* (wretched, miserable) and *"cor"* (heart). In other words *"misericordia"* translated in English as mercy literally means the heart that is drawn to misery or a miserable situation—it is our miserable state that catches the attention of our loving Father. The Sacred Heart is always drawn to a humble, contrite but miserable heart. And in their misery, these two

3 Cf. FRANCIS, Apostolic Letter *Misericordia et Misera* (20 November 2016)

women attracted the heart of Jesus. Pope Francis captures it beautifully: "the misery of sin was clothed with the mercy of love."[4]

My experience as a confessor has taught me a lesson that I believe many who come before a priest in the confessional must know. It would seem that hearing the confession of someone would make you see how terrible they are, but often I experienced the contrary; I realized how holy they are; how deeply wounded they are because they have offended the one they love. Let us cast our minds to the encounter between the woman who had a bad name (Luke 7:36-50) and Jesus. "Therefore, I tell you, her many sins have been forgiven—as her great love has shown" (vs 47)—this statement speaks volumes considered within the context of the parable Jesus narrated[5] and later what he would indicate as the greatest commandment of all. Not only did Jesus declare this woman forgiven, but within the context of "confession" she was declared a saint—she had great love. To be a saint is to love, and to be a great saint is to love greatly. A priest who listens in the manner of Jesus does not so much see the evil done by the penitent but the love that brought him or her to Jesus. If you want to know the impression you leave on priests who listen to your confession, this is mainly it.

Then I discovered how as a priest I recognize myself as a sinner and identify with the penitent. In the confessional as a dispenser of grace, my weaknesses are revealed, and I recognize my own thirst for healing and mercy. Saint Paul could not have indicated this in any other way but to say:

---

[4] Ibid, no.1.

[5] "'Two people owed money to a certain moneylender. One owed him five hundred denarii,[a] and the other fifty. Neither of them had the money to pay him back, so he forgave the debts of both. Now which of them will love him more?' Simon answered, 'The one who was let off more, I suppose." Jesus said, "You are right." (Luke 7:40-43)

"But we hold this treasure in pots of earthenware, so that the immensity of the power is God's and not our own" (2 Cor. 4:7).

Finally, it is the joy of imagining the Father's love and being the sacrament of the embrace of the Father (cf. Luke 15:21). I personally love to be touched by the priest who absolves me because his touch becomes for me the sacramental touch of the Father. Touch is always a symbol of affection and love, and when I hear those words: "I absolve you in the name of the Father and of the Son and of the Holy Spirit," I know my sins have been forgiven. There is a great sense of joy knowing that through you God grants healing and forgiveness to many. We come to the Lord in the sacrament broken and go back with hope of living in love: we come in tears and go back comforted; we come wounded and we go back healed—all because Jesus promised that whose sins you forgive, they are forgiven, and whose sins you retain, they are retained.

My Encounter with the Mercy of God in the Light of *Misericordiae Vultus*

Rev. Fr. Francis Destiny Amenuvor

It gives me so much delight to contribute this note to this tremendous book by Rev. Fr. Aaron Agorsor. A few years ago, precisely in 2016, Pope Francis led the universal Church in observing the Extraordinary Jubilee Year hinged on the theme: "Be Merciful as Your Heavenly Father is Merciful" (Luke 6:38). I believe that this Pastoral plan led by the Holy Father was so opportune at this particular era in the Church's life when the sins of the Church committed in the past are being exposed and reparations being demanded.

In the little document *Misericordiae Vultus* (the face of Mercy) issued to explain and guide the celebration of the extraordinary jubilee year, the Holy Father states in no uncertain terms that the Father never tires of showing mercy.

As a priest mandated to steer the celebration of the Jubilee of Mercy in the Archdiocese of Accra in Ghana, West Africa, I found the period so intriguing. As a local Church, certain Churches, Shrines and grottoes were designated as places of indulgence, and awareness was created in those places about the extraordinary Jubilee. The Holy Door was cited at the Holy Spirit Cathedral, and scores of people exercised faith in going through the Holy Door with its accompanying spiritual exercises. The sacrament of reconciliation was better appreciated by the clergy and laity of the Church and many more people availed themselves to a more meaningful celebration of this sacrament.

On my personal spiritual and faith journey, I discovered that the celebration of the extraordinary Jubilee of Mercy had sharpened my consciousness about the devastation of sin and a life of sin and at the same time had enhanced my hope for a restoration of the sinner which has so much inspired my journey of reparation. The truth is that instead of brooding over our past sins and mistakes, every child of God redeemed by the saving action of Jesus Christ should focus on his or her journey of reparation so as to lay hold on eternal life. We can only make it to heaven because we have been beneficiaries of Divine Mercy and Divine Grace.

TAKING MY SEAT IN THE GALLERY OF HONOUR

Raymond Tuvi, AMDG, rtuvi2000@yahoo.com

Just a Step Away From Destruction

The steadfast Love of the Lord never ceases; His Mercies never come to an end; they are new every morning; great is your Faithfulness (Lamentations 3:22-23)

In my latest post, I shared how the blessing and favour of God that enabled me to meet and interact with the Speaker of the U.S. House of Representatives, Nancy Pelosi, in Accra was likely occasioned by acts of charity we have been involved in over some time–notably visiting an orphanage a few days before, as well as preparing Parliamentary legislation for the responsible care for all children in Ghana.

But while this could be a true cause and effect sequence, because God considers doing those acts of charity pure and genuine religion (James 1:27), I could still have been speculating as to what actually moved/moves God's hand to bless us as He did/does. I may, in reality, have already earned His favour for that blessing and more, for that singular act of charity–and more. This is because, while I could have forgotten about that orphanage visit because of the series of difficulties I encountered just before it occurred, and because I also had to go get some prescribed medication for my octogenarian mother round about the same time, I opted to hold on awhile and make the orphanage experience a reality, and a fulfilling one at that.

Even though I may have secured my place in the "gallery of honour" (I was probably the youngest and perhaps least publicly visible among the dignitaries in the Public Gallery of Parliament that day), an event that occurred the morning I was going for my invitation at Parliament put me "just a step away from destruction," so to speak. That event and the outcome of eventually meeting the U.S. House of Reps Speaker the next day has given me a new perspective that our success isn't as much about our efforts as it is about God's mercy. (It is also called Grace, oftentimes.)

Because, as I was on my way to Parliament to secure my invitation after that unfortunate incident at home, many clear signs showed me that I had fallen short of God's glory (i.e. sinned) and was veritably on the wrong side of His approval. It didn't matter that that incident was occasioned by the coming to a head of the actions of a relative who contributes zilch to domestic resources for bills yet prevents the entry into our apartment of domestic helps to help take care of Mom.

I had had it up to the forehead; and though I was allowed by instincts to, for the first time in a number of years, voice my frustration, I might have gone slightly overboard in expressing my justified reservations to an older relative.

The first sign of anomaly was Mom's rare remonstration against discord between blood relations. The second was perceived as a mischievous look by a normally reticent tenant, as I went downstairs to bid Mom and others bye for the day: I sharply questioned that "*konkonsa*" expression, though.

The clearest sign of breach of Divine favour came as I stepped out of the house, making for the car to take me to Parliament House: A highly-unkempt, hideous-looking man was just a step away from crossing my path. That was just not normal. But, thanks be to God, the day was saved.

In the car and on the way, the usual signs and signals (of the Holy Spirit) that guide were all around again; but this time, the majority were unusual, in that they were clear and sharp in questioning the excessive reaction to the errant relative's attitude. As I got the message and went into remorseful and suppliant mode, a message on a *trotro* that tenderly said, "Merciful God," appeared and reappeared a number of times on the route, leading me till I was certain of God's merciful intervention. I felt that within and all around me.

I hardly anticipated such mercifulness of God in doldrums as those. Yet, in *The Name of God is Mercy* (Pan Macmillan, 2017), an exploration on the universal theme of mercy, Pope Francis tells us that: "The first and only step required to experience mercy is to acknowledge that we are in need of mercy. Jesus comes for us, when we recognize that we are sinners." So, I thanked God heartily for His immeasurable love thus expressed.

That, about just an hour after that loving embrace of God's mercy, I got, by a series of freely opening doors, my invitation to Speaker Pelosi's visit and address to Ghana's Legislature (at the head of a twelve-member U.S. Congressional Black Caucus Delegation visiting as part of Ghana's Year of Return in commemoration of the 400th anniversary of the landing of the first enslaved Africans in the United States)–and my subsequent memorable interaction and photo-op with her–is ample testament to God's immense mercy to me when I least expected it.

What amazing love! Merciful is what the Father is!

Rev. Fr. James Ahenkorah
(Iowa USA, 2019).
April 2016

Bless the Lord, O my soul, and all that is within me, bless his holy name! Bless the Lord, O my soul, and forget not all his benefits, who forgives all your iniquity, who heals all your diseases, who redeems your life from the pit, who crowns you with steadfast love and mercy, who satisfies you with good so that your youth is renewed like the eagle's. (Psalm 103:1-5)

The above psalm is a vivid reminder of God's steadfast love towards me. Indeed His mercies never come to an end, they are new every morning. (Cf. Lamentations 3:22-23). I feel very blessed, and I am eternally grateful to God for the gift of my life and ministry. To put it bluntly, but for God's grace and mercy, I shouldn't be walking in this land of the living. This testimony that I share with you is just one of the many instances in which God spared my life not because of any righteous deed or any merits of mine but out of His extravagant love for an unworthy servant. With all the near-death experiences that I have had, I have come to this realization that I am still walking the surface of this earth because God created me with a purpose and has given me a mission to accomplish. Pray with me, will you? that as I share this testimony many who will read this book authored by Rev. Fr. Aaron Agorsor will come to the saving knowledge of Christ and experience His amazing grace and mercy.

It all happened on the morning of the 18th day of September, 2017. Jordan and Leslie Cimeni, a Filipino couple in my parish, St. John in Greenfield, Iowa, had prearranged for us to visit the Grotto of the redemption in West Bend, Iowa, USA. We said a prayer for God's traveling mercies for ourselves and other road users, put in a gospel CD, and started our journey a few minutes after 8:00 am. I sat in the front seat, Jordan was the driver, and Leslie was in the back seat right behind me. We sang along some of the gospel music playing and talked about some of the chords used in the music. Jordan is an amazing guitarist, vocalist, and songwriter. We also talked about pilgrimages, parish life and some other theological issues including exorcisms. As we continued on our journey with our conversations, it started drizzling, and in no time it was raining heavily making visibility quite poor. Not before long, we were at Fort Dodge and quite close to West Bend which was our destination. It was at one of the intersections at Fort Dodge that suddenly a pickup truck T-boned our Mitsubishi saloon car.

A few minutes before the near fatal accident, Leslie who was sitting right behind me in the back seat had moved from where she was to the middle seat. Apparently, there was a stop sign for us, but due to the heavy rain and the poor visibility Jordan did not see it and so went straight into the intersection. We were hit by the pickup driver who had the right of way. Just before the impact, all I felt was a certain calmness and peace that words cannot explain. It felt as if I was in different world. I saw everything up to the impact and must have passed out just for a little while and regained consciousness because I saw and could recall all that happened afterwards. Within a few minutes the first responder was by our car. He was a policeman. He managed to open one of the side doors and believe you me his first words were "Jesus please save them, Jesus please help them." He then asked a few questions, I guess to keep us conscious or most probably as part of the routine checks as we waited for the ambulance. All the airbags in the car had gone off. I was stuck in my seat. I felt some numbness in my feet and sharp pain in my neck and chest. Jordan, managed to get out of the car to check on Leslie who was also stuck in the back seat and laid unconscious. Our side of the car was hit. She came back briefly, and I managed to say the words of absolution for Jordan and Leslie. In no time, the ambulance had arrived with the paramedics. With their sophisticated equipment they managed to cut the doors and get us out of the vehicle. I remember telling the police officer to call for a Catholic priest. This same policeman who had prayed with us entered the ambulance and wrapped a rosary that was hanging in the car around my right wrist.

We were taken to the Methodist hospital in Fort Dodge. Msgr. McQuaid, the vicar general of the diocese of Davenport, was at the hospital to pray with us and anoint us. In fact, that was all I was waiting for so I could sing my

"Nunc Dimitis." All this while my neck had been braced and I had been confined to a bed and could make only a few movements as I was being prepared to have a full body MRI scan. I later learned that Leslie was airlifted from Fort Dodge to the Methodist hospital in Des Moines, Iowa. Fast forward, the scan came out good. I had a contusion of my chest, some lacerations on my neck from the seat belt, some pain in my back and waist. I was discharged that same day, and Rev. Fr. Raphael Assamah, pastor of St. Mary, Shenandoah, a priest from the Archdiocese of Accra, Ghana, with whom I am on secondment in the diocese of Des Moines drove for about four hours to see me at the hospital and bring me home when I was discharged. I had to see a chiropractor for a couple of weeks, but thankfully I had no permanent injuries. Leslie had suffered some broken ribs and some pain in the neck. Jordan complained only of some bodily pains and aches. With a matter of weeks we were all moving about again thanks to God's grace and mercy. One thing the doctor on duty that fateful day said which I will always remember as long as live was "someone up there was looking after you guys." The car was totally wrecked, and all who saw it were amazed to hear all three people on board survived the accident.

This accident and other near death encounters I have had, like nearly getting drowned in the sea on two occasions, have served and continue to serve as memorial markers that remind me of God's unique love for me. Then Samuel took a stone and set it up between Mizpah and Shen. He named it Ebenezer, saying, "Thus far the LORD has helped us" (1 Samuel 7:12).

WHERE I FOUND FORGIVENESS
Andrews Obeng, SVD

I was seventeen years old and battling with guilt. I needed someone to talk to and help me offload the burden of sin. It happened that a young bearded priest in spectacles, Fr. Charles Pokoo, came to our school for a day's recollection, and the opportunity was given for Confession. He wore a white cassock with a purple stole. One by one, those who desired to access the grace of reconciliation and make peace with their conscience ascended that sacred space where he sat. As I awaited my turn, I rehearsed meticulously what to say, "Bless me Father for I have sinned. It has been...since my last confession. My sins are..."

My hour finally came and with great trepidation I went and sat before him. He welcomed me with glittering eyes and a broad smile. That warm expression of love on his face was enough to chase away the fear that was lurking in my soul. As I confessed my sins, I wondered intermittently what may be running through his mind. When I was done, I waited for his verdict. He looked at me and smiled even more broadly and then proceeded to tell me how deep is the love of God. He offered me a bible text to pray with as my penance and invited me to say a prayer of contrition. Then raising his right hand slightly above my head, he uttered the words of absolution and tears of deep inner peace mingled with joy rolled down my cheeks. Speaking 'in nomine Christi' he said to me, "Go in peace, your sins have been forgiven." I responded with a note of thanksgiving and walked out of the confessional as light as a feather.

That day, I encountered Jesus Christ through the ministry of a Catholic priest. That encounter was a lifeline for me. Thanks to the grace I found, here am I, now a minister of that same grace to other people. That tangible experience of mercy in my life buttresses a point Pope Francis made: "The mercy of God is not an abstract idea, but a concrete reality with which he reveals his love as of that of a father or mother, moved to the very depths out of love for their child. It is hardly an exaggeration to say that this is a "visceral" love. It gushes forth from the depths naturally, full of tenderness and compassion, indulgence and mercy" (*MV*, 6).

In my ministry as a priest, I consider myself a dispenser of God's mercy. After close to 15 years of absolving the sins of penitents in the Sacrament of Recollection, I have come to believe that there is no sin greater than the Mercy of God.

CONCLUSION

It is said that copying is the highest form of praise. Many have written very impressive and powerful reflections on mercy. What I have done is just a drop in the ocean. But my consolation is that the ocean cannot be complete without the drop. I turn my gaze on priests, the dispensers of God mercy. What kind of priest should the faithful turn to in their challenging moments? What kind of priest will the world of today turn to? These mind boggling but relevant and timely questions must be answered today by the priests in the Third Millennium, especially in the face of the abuses and scandals that have hit and continue to cause havoc to the leadership of the Church.

At a time that Christ's faithful are hurt and wounded because of these abuses and scandals and the many who have lost faith, abandoned or contemplating abandoning the Church, this book offers hope to the remnant of the Church so that they will become that light to dispel the darkness of sin and doubt in people's mind about the priests and the Church. The fact that a priest is called to be a man of mercy, joyful and a faithful minister, a shepherd who has "the smell of the sheep"—above all, with a heart centered on Christ and the Sacraments—gives me hope. This is what Pope Francis assures us of in his book *Men of Mercy*. Through these, Pope Francis offers wisdom and encouragement to all priests. He knows the demands we face and how tired and discouraged we can become especially during this period of abuses and scandals within the leadership of the Church. We priests need mercy, too, as anybody else, and the only way to give this mercy out is to open up to experience this mercy ourselves and confidently and faithfully spread this message with joy, hope, and authenticity. The Holy Father says:

> May mercy guide our steps, inspire our reforms, and enlighten our decisions. May it be the basis of all our efforts. May it teach us when to move forward and when to step back. May it also enable us to understand the littleness of all that we do in God's greater plan of salvation and his majestic and mysterious working.

We, all must work toward restoring the image and dignity of the Priesthood. In the image of the Good Shepherd, the priest is a man of mercy and compassion, close to his people and a servant to all. Pope Francis in his book *Men of Mercy* re-echoes this sentiment:

> The mercy of our God is infinite and indescribable. We express the power of this mystery as an ever "ever greater" mercy, a mercy in motion, a mercy that each day seeks to make progress, taking small steps forward and advancing in the wasteland where indifference and violence have predominated. (p. 26)

We live in a world where apathy, violence, and the like seem to be the order of the day. In face of terrorism, for instance, we need to step forward as ambassadors of God's infinite mercy. Sometimes, we are angry in the face of terrorist attacks and wish to retaliate. The reality is that those perpetrating these heinous crimes are our brothers and sisters. The story of the Good Samaritan is one practical way God expects us to become the face of his mercy. In the face of racial discrimination existing between Jews and Samaritans, the Good Samaritan showed that mercy transcends race, color, ethnicity, and the like. In fact, mercy makes us brothers and sisters and servants to one another. Instead of giving excuses like the priests and Levites did when they encountered the man who fell to the thieves, we should become bearers of the mercy of God which tears down the walls of division, religious codes, and doctrines that have the potential of denying people the mercy of God. God's mercy never goes waste in so far as it restores the dignity of the human person. The Holy Father adds in *Men of Mercy*,

> It is good for us to break out of our set ways, because it is proper to the Heart of God to overflow with tenderness, with ever more to give. For the Lord prefers something to be wasted rather than one drop of mercy be held back. He would rather have many seeds carried off by the birds of the air than have one seed missing, since each of those seeds has the capacity to bear abundant fruit, thirtyfold, sixtyfold, even hundredfold. (pp. 26-27)

There is no despair in witnessing to mercy even though acknowledging that we are sinners often brings us shame, at the same time, it restores dignity to the human person. That is why I agree with no stretch of doubt Pope Francis' call on all priests in *Men of Mercy*:

> As priests, we are witnesses to and minister of the ever increasing abundance of the Father's mercy; we have the rewarding and consoling task of incarnating mercy, as Jesus did, who "went about doing good and healing"(Acts 10:38) in thousand ways so that each person can embrace it and experience it personally. This will help all people truly understand and practice mercy with

> creativity, in ways that respect their local cultures and families (p. 27).

In addressing the parishioners of the Cathedral of the Transfiguration of Our Lord, Palo, Saturday, 17 January 2015 after the devastation caused by Typhoon Yolanda, Pope Francis said the following:

> … I hope that you will always realize that true happiness comes from helping others, giving ourselves to them in self-sacrifice, mercy and compassion. In this way you will be a powerful force for the renewal of society, not only in the work of restoring buildings but more importantly, in building up God's kingdom of holiness, justice and peace in your native land (*Men of Mercy*, 89-90).

I think that in the light of the Holy Father's comment above, being merciful to people goes beyond just putting up a building for them; more importantly, it is about restoring dignity and hope. The story of Jesus' encounter with the blind man Bartimaeus reveals in no uncertain terms the two natures of the Church as wounded and at the same time a healer. I wish to reiterate again that Jesus was on his way to Jerusalem to face death when he encountered Bartimaeus. Jesus, though a Divine Person, had a human nature, so there were many things going on in his mind. In fact, he was broken in the face of his imminent death. Then following him was a thick crowd listening to his message of salvation. Finally, this blind man Bartimaeus, whom everyone else despised, wanted Jesus' attention. In his brokenness and woundedness, Jesus heard the cry of Bartimaeus when everyone else despised him. He stopped to have him brought to him and the simple question he posed to Bartimaeus was "What can I do for you?" We need grace to be like Jesus who though wounded brought healing to Bartimaeus. There are a lot of Bartimaeuses around us who want to see Jesus in us in order to turn to us. Ministry is not better offered or carried out in the comfort of our mission houses or Churches. Ministry is out there: on the street corners, in the slums, in the market places, in our offices, in our schools, and everywhere else human beings gather. Ministry is better exercised when we are wounded.

Two major characters feature prominently in this book as regards the mercy of God: Zacchaeus and Bartimaeus. Zacchaeus represents the rich, the powerful in society who need God's mercy, while Bartimaeus represents the poor, the despised, and the vulnerable in society who need God's mercy, too.

The Gospel of Lk 19:1-10 is a story of Zacchaeus the Chief Tax Collector. Zacchaeus' name means righteous. This is a paradox because, he did not live up to his name. He is also a Chief Tax Collector. This detail is interesting. He is not like Levi (Matthew who is just a tax collector). The Greek word ARCHITELŌNĒS means the "arch-tax collector," the chief of all the tax collectors. Jesus was passing through Jericho. First, Jericho is like a border town. It is the first town one comes across crossing the Jordan from Transjordan towards Jerusalem. It is a big tax collection point. Second, if one is approaching Jerusalem from the North, from Galilee through Samaria, one is likely to pass through Jericho. So it is a big thing that he is chief of the tax collectors there. Simply put, Zacchaeus is a public figure.

But the account indicates in Lk 19:3-4 that Zacchaeus wanted to see Jesus. The remark seems casual until we begin to look closely. The first thing is the verb HORAŌ (to see) which Luke uses. This verb denotes more than casual sight. In fact in Lk 19:5 when Jesus looks up the tree to see Zacchaeus, Luke uses a different verb ANABLEPŌ, that means to look in a very ordinary sense. Zacchaeus however needed to SEE JESUS in a much deeper sense. So why did he need to see Jesus? I suggest three challenges Zacchaeus had. The first is that he had a physical impediment, he was short (MIKROS). We are not unfamiliar with the crowds in Jericho, and how they treat people with physical challenges. The preceding passage in Lk 18:35-43 recounts the story of a blind man in the same town of Jericho, the same one whom Mark calls Bartimaeus (Mk 10:46). The crowds shouted the latter down; now, they wouldn't give the short Zacchaeus a chance. If you were disabled, Jericho was not your place of choice.

Zacchaeus had a second problem. Remember that the blind Bartimaeus was a poor beggar. Not Zacchaeus! He was filthy rich. But there is something curious in the account. Ordinarily, if a rich man wanted to see Jesus, wouldn't everyone just step back and allow him? The same Luke tells the story of a certain centurion in Lk 7:1-10. This man is a pagan and yet when his SLAVE is ill, the Jewish elders in a long file go to entreat Jesus to go to his house. Why? Because he built them a synagogue. But Zacchaeus is a Jew, yet not even the poor on the street have any regard for him. No one recognises him. Even when Jesus eventually agrees to go to his house, the people murmur. The term Luke uses to describe Zacchaeus is HĒLIKIA (stature). He was small in HĒLIKIA. But this is more than just a physical attribute. Socially, he was small. He had tried to buy influence with money. It failed! He had all the wealth but no human dignity. That is how the richest man in town needed to climb a tree like small boys do. Zacchaeus had no dignity even among the poor of Jericho.

The third problem Zacchaeus had was spiritual. He was a tax-collector, a collaborator with the Romans, a traitor! Zacchaeus could not have entered the temple. He was practically excommunicated. It is interesting reading what Jesus told him in Greek. He says in Lk 19:5, Zacchaeus, hurry and come down. IT IS NECESSARY FOR ME TO STAY IN YOUR HOUSE TODAY or I MUST STAY IN YOUR HOUSE TODAY. Why is it necessary for Jesus to stay in his house? Well, because Zacchaeus, like the centurion of Lk 7 is barred from God's house. He cannot go to God's House; God must come to him.

What is interesting is the transformation that takes place when Jesus enters Zacchaeus' house. Remember that Jesus has not given prior notice. Everything is as it normally is. Zacchaeus allows Jesus to see his inner situation just as he is. So does he receive his request to SEE Jesus? Yes he does. What Zacchaeus sees is quite interesting and revealing. When he sees Jesus, it opens up his eyes to see the poor. One thing Zacchaeus had never SEEN before were poor people. For him, they didn't exist. All that mattered was money. Now for the first time his eyes and his heart are open to the poor. He can now perceive the beggar on the road. He is now going to give half his money to the poor. The other half he is going to use to pay all those whom he had defrauded. Zacchaeus' eyes have been opened but interestingly he saw Jesus where he did not expect him to be, in the poor! If you were the only rich person in the world, Jesus comes in search of you so that he shows you mercy so that through you many more experience the infinite love of God.

Bartimaeus, on the other hand, a poor, despised man; a blind beggar. Unlike Zacchaeus, he offends no one. He is despised by virtue of the fact that he is poor and blind. He was also vulnerable; he needed a shoulder to cry on. Like Zacchaeus, he thinks meeting Jesus is his last resort and he breaks all protocol, despising what everyone else says and starts shouting even before a thick crowd; even before an impossible impenetrable crowd. Again, like Jesus finds

Zacchaeus, he finds Bartimaeus, too. Jesus hears the shout and call of a poor beggar even in the midst of a thick crowd and responds to a man despised; a nobody. Mercy finds even when human strength fails. Jesus Christ, the face of the God's mercy, found Bartimaeus. Two times, Bartimaeus makes a distress call to Jesus to have mercy on him. This is very profound and timing: "Jesus, Son of David, Have mercy on me" (Mk. 10:47-48). Bartimaeus does not only have his physical sight restored but he becomes a man of faith symbolized in throwing off his cloaks. Bartimaeus is now a new creation; the old order is gone. Having encountered mercy, Bartimaeus becomes a missionary and a disciple of Jesus.

The things common to both Zacchaeus and Bartimaeus are that they are both vulnerable and needed God's mercy. Both are despised by all manner of people, and they both long for a savior. God's mercy is a panacea for both the rich and the poor; the powerful and the despised. Zacchaeus and Bartimaeus represent these divide.

Now I turn my gaze on the identity of the Catholic Priesthood as dispensers of God's unfathomable mercy. In the Decree on the Ministry and Life of Priests (*Presbyterorum Ordinis*), the Fathers of the Second Vatican Council says:

> The Priest shares in the authority by which Christ himself builds up, sanctifies, and rules his body. Therefore... the sacerdotal office... is conferred by that special sacrament through which priests, by anointing of the Holy Spirit, are marked with a special character and are so configured to Christ the Priest that they can act in the person of Christ the Head. (No.2)

Our duty as priests are three fold: sanctify, teach and

govern the people of God entrusted to us. Cardinal Dolan in his book, *Priests for the Third Millennium*, says this of the priesthood: "The priesthood is a call, not a career, a redefinition of self, not just a new ministry; a way of life, not a job; a state of being, not just a function; a permanent, lifelong commitment, not a temporary style of service; an identity, not just a role" (p. 228). It is these attributes that the priest in the Third Millennium must possess in order to face the challenges of priesthood today. Our fidelity is proven in the face of adversity. St. Teresa of Calcutta once said, "God did not call us to be successful but to be faithful. If there was any time the Church requires our fidelity, it is now; in the midst of the scandals. If there were any time in the life of a priest that the prayer of St. Thomas Aquinas is still relevant, it is now:

> Give me, O Lord, a steadfast heart which no unworthy affection may drag downwards
> Give me an unconquered heart which no tribulation can wear out
> Give me an upright heart which no unworthy purpose may tempt aside.
> Bestow on me, O Lord my God, a faithfulness that may finally embrace you.

Our faithfulness to the sacrament of penance is more urgent than before. This is the hope of the Church. My experience in sitting in the confessional for seven years has taught me many lessons about the Sacrament of Penance and the penitents. Some penitents come already despaired to the extent that they become scrupulous. Some come confessing the same sins over and over again. Others come frustrated because they have prayed and done all that you have told them to do but still battle with their weaknesses, sins and doubts. Sometimes, they wish to sleep and wake and their weaknesses are all gone. These moments can be very challenging and frustrating for priests to the extent that many dread sitting in the confessional to hear confession. Our duty is to give them hope. I think that it is in the confessional that I feel more *in persona Christi*. This humbles me. I think, if every priest is given the opportunity, they will say the same thing. We must remember that the sacrament works in spite of us. The grace of God's mercy flows through us. Cardinal Dolan says this of the sacrament of Penance in *Priests for the Third Millennium*:

> So it is that the major message we proclaim in the beautiful sacrament is not a proposition, not advice, but a person: we proclaim Christ! As confessors, we are not theologians, although...a good sound of moral theology, is called for. As confessors, we are not psychologists, although insights from that helpful discipline are valuable. As confessors, we are not social workers...As confessors, we are Christ, and so the major thing we say is, "Our Lord loves you very much; Jesus now completely forgives all your sins; your sorrow for sins moves his Sacred Heart; heaven is rejoicing because you have returned; Jesus is happy because you have accepted his invitation to repent and have made his cross worthwhile; Jesus never loves us more than when we tell him we're sorry. (p. 244)

As confessors, we must be Jesus to the penitent. The penitent comes already broken like Zacchaeus and Bartimaeus. They do not need condemnation but love, for we are not judges or arbitrators in the confessional but instruments of God's mercy. Pope Francis reminds us in Apostolic Exaltation, *Evangelii Gaudium* (Joy of the Gospel) that the confessional is a not a torture chamber, but rather an encounter with the Lord's mercy; it is a place where God waits for us. God is a father and he is always waiting for us! It is so wonderful to feel the merciful embrace of the father in the Sacrament of Reconciliation, to discover that the confessional is a place of mercy.

May all who read this book rediscover anew the unfathomable Divine Mercy. I would like to conclude with the opening and closing prayer of the Chaplet of Divine Mercy which I recommend for my penitents and draw strength from in my sinful moments:

> You expired, Jesus, but the source of life gushed forth for souls, and the ocean of mercy opened up for the whole world. O Fount of Life, unfathomable Divine Mercy, envelop the whole world and empty Yourself out upon us. O Blood and Water, which gushed forth from the Heart of Jesus as a fount of mercy for us, I trust in You!

To all penitents including me I offer the concluding prayer of the Chaplet of Divine Mercy:

> Eternal God, in whom mercy is endless and treasury of compassion-inexhaustible, look kindly upon us and increase Your mercy in us, that in difficult moments we might not despair nor become despondent, but with great confidence submit ourselves to Your holy will, which is Love and Mercy itself.

APPENDIX

Misericordiae Vultus

BULL OF INDICTION
OF THE EXTRAORDINARY
JUBILEE OF MERCY

FRANCIS
BISHOP OF ROME
SERVANT OF THE SERVANTS OF GOD
TO ALL WHO READ THIS LETTER
GRACE, MERCY, AND PEACE

1. Jesus Christ is the face of the Father's mercy. These words might well sum up the mystery of the Christian faith. Mercy has become living and visible in Jesus of Nazareth, reaching its culmination in him. The Father, "rich in mercy" (Eph 2:4), after having revealed his name to Moses as "a God merciful and gracious, slow to anger, and abounding in steadfast love and faithfulness" (Ex 34:6), has never ceased to show, in various ways throughout history, his divine nature. In the "fullness of time" (Gal 4:4), when everything had been arranged according to his plan of salvation, he sent his only Son into the world, born of the Virgin Mary, to reveal his love for us in a definitive way. Whoever sees Jesus sees the Father (cf. Jn 14:9). Jesus of Nazareth, by his words,

his actions, and his entire person[1] reveals the mercy of God.

2. We need constantly to contemplate the mystery of mercy. It is a wellspring of joy, serenity, and peace. Our salvation depends on it. Mercy: the word reveals the very mystery of the Most Holy Trinity. Mercy: the ultimate and supreme act by which God comes to meet us. Mercy: the fundamental law that dwells in the heart of every person who looks sincerely into the eyes of his brothers and sisters on the path of life. Mercy: the bridge that connects God and man, opening our hearts to the hope of being loved forever despite our sinfulness.

3. At times we are called to gaze even more attentively on mercy so that we may become a more effective sign of the Father's action in our lives. For this reason I have proclaimed an Extraordinary Jubilee of Mercy as a special time for the Church, a time when the witness of believers might grow stronger and more effective.

The Holy Year will open on 8 December 2015, the Solemnity of the Immaculate Conception. This liturgical feast day recalls God's action from the very beginning of the history of mankind. After the sin of Adam and Eve, God did not wish to leave humanity alone in the throes of evil. And so he turned his gaze to Mary, holy and immaculate in love (cf. Eph 1:4), choosing her to be the Mother of man's Redeemer. When faced with the gravity of sin, God responds with the fullness of mercy. Mercy will always be greater than any sin, and no one can place limits on the love of God who is ever ready to forgive. I will have the joy of opening the Holy Door on the Solemnity of the Immaculate Conception. On that day, the Holy Door will become a Door of Mercy through which anyone who enters will experience the love of God who consoles, pardons, and instils hope.

On the following Sunday, the Third Sunday of Advent, the Holy Door of the Cathedral of Rome – that is, the Basilica of Saint John Lateran – will be opened. In the following weeks, the Holy Doors of the other Papal Basilicas will be opened. On the same Sunday, I will announce that in every local church, at the cathedral – the mother church of the faithful in any particular area – or, alternatively, at the co-cathedral or another church of special significance, a Door of Mercy will be opened for the duration of the Holy Year. At the discretion of the local ordinary, a similar door may be opened at any shrine frequented by large groups of pilgrims, since visits to these holy sites are so often grace-filled moments, as people discover a path to conversion. Every Particular Church, therefore, will be directly involved in living out this Holy Year as an extraordinary moment of grace and spiritual renewal. Thus the Jubilee will be celebrated both in Rome and in the Particular Churches as a visible sign of the Church's universal communion.

4. I have chosen the date of 8 December because of its rich meaning in the recent history of the Church. In fact, I will open the Holy Door on the fiftieth anniversary of the closing of the Second Vatican Ecumenical Council. The Church feels a great need to keep this event alive. With the Council, the Church entered a new phase of her history. The Council Fathers strongly perceived, as a true breath of the Holy Spirit, a need to talk about God to men and women of their time in a more accessible way. The walls which for too long had made the Church a kind of fortress were torn down and the time had come to proclaim the Gospel in a new way. It was a new phase of the same evangelization that had existed from the beginning. It was a fresh undertaking for all Christians to bear witness to their faith with greater enthusiasm and conviction. The Church sensed a

responsibility to be a living sign of the Father's love in the world.

We recall the poignant words of Saint John XXIII when, opening the Council, he indicated the path to follow: "Now the Bride of Christ wishes to use the medicine of mercy rather than taking up arms of severity... The Catholic Church, as she holds high the torch of Catholic truth at this Ecumenical Council, wants to show herself a loving mother to all; patient, kind, moved by compassion and goodness toward her separated children".[2] Blessed Paul VI spoke in a similar vein at the closing of the Council: "We prefer to point out how charity has been the principal religious feature of this Council... the old story of the Good Samaritan has been the model of the spirituality of the Council... a wave of affection and admiration flowed from the Council over the modern world of humanity. Errors were condemned, indeed, because charity demanded this no less than did truth, but for individuals themselves there was only admonition, respect and love. Instead of depressing diagnoses, encouraging remedies; instead of direful predictions, messages of trust issued from the Council to the present-day world. The modern world's values were not only respected but honoured, its efforts approved, its aspirations purified and blessed... Another point we must stress is this: all this rich teaching is channelled in one direction, the service of mankind, of every condition, in every weakness and need".[3]

With these sentiments of gratitude for everything the Church has received, and with a sense of responsibility for the task that lies ahead, we shall cross the threshold of the Holy Door fully confident that the strength of the Risen Lord, who constantly supports us on our pilgrim way, will sustain us. May the Holy Spirit, who guides the steps of believers in cooperating with the work of salvation wrought by Christ, lead the way and support the People of God so that they may contemplate the face of mercy.[4]

5. The Jubilee year will close with the liturgical Solemnity of Christ the King on 20 November 2016. On that day, as we seal the Holy Door, we shall be filled, above all, with a sense of gratitude and thanksgiving to the Most Holy Trinity for having granted us an extraordinary time of grace. We will entrust the life of the Church, all humanity, and the entire cosmos to the Lordship of Christ, asking him to pour out his mercy upon us like the morning dew, so that everyone may work together to build a brighter future. How much I desire that the year to come will be steeped in mercy, so that we can go out to every man and woman, bringing the goodness and tenderness of God! May the balm of mercy reach everyone, both believers and those far away, as a sign that the Kingdom of God is already present in our midst!

6. "It is proper to God to exercise mercy, and he manifests his omnipotence particularly in this way".[5] Saint Thomas Aquinas' words show that God's mercy, rather than a sign of weakness, is the mark of his omnipotence. For this reason the liturgy, in one of its most ancient collects, has us pray: "O God, who reveal your power above all in your mercy and forgiveness ..."[6] Throughout the history of humanity, God will always be the One who is present, close, provident, holy, and merciful.

"Patient and merciful." These words often go together in the Old Testament to describe God's nature. His being merciful is concretely demonstrated in his many actions throughout the history of salvation where his goodness prevails over punishment and destruction. In a special way the Psalms bring to the fore the grandeur of his merciful action: "He forgives all your iniquity, he heals all your diseases, he redeems your life from the pit, he crowns you with steadfast love and mercy" (Ps 103:3-4). Another psalm, in an even more explicit way, attests to the concrete signs of his mercy: "He executes justice for the oppressed; he gives food to the hungry. The Lord sets the prisoners free; the Lord opens the eyes of the blind. The Lord lifts up those who are bowed down; the Lord loves the righteous. The Lord watches over the sojourners, he upholds the widow and the fatherless; but the way of the wicked he brings to ruin" (Ps 146:7-9). Here are some other expressions of the Psalmist: "He heals the brokenhearted, and binds up their wounds... The Lord lifts up the downtrodden, he casts the wicked to the ground" (Ps 147:3, 6). In short, the mercy of God is not an abstract idea, but a concrete reality with which he reveals his love as of that of a father or a mother, moved to the very depths out of love for their child. It is hardly an exaggeration to say that this is a "visceral" love. It gushes forth from the depths naturally, full of tenderness and compassion, indulgence and mercy.

7. "For his mercy endures forever." This is the refrain that repeats after each verse in Psalm 136 as it narrates the history of God's revelation. By virtue of mercy, all the events of the Old Testament are replete with profound salvific import. Mercy renders God's history with Israel a history of salvation. To repeat continually "for his mercy endures forever," as the psalm does, seems to break through the dimensions of space and time, inserting everything into the eternal mystery of love. It is as if to say that not only in history, but for all eternity man will always be under the merciful gaze of the Father. It is no accident that the people of Israel wanted to include this psalm – the "Great Hallel," as it is called – in its most important liturgical feast days.

Before his Passion, Jesus prayed with this psalm of mercy. Matthew attests to this in his Gospel when he says that, "when they had sung a hymn" (26:30), Jesus and his disciples went out to the Mount of Olives. While he was instituting the Eucharist as an everlasting memorial of himself and his paschal sacrifice, he symbolically placed this supreme act of revelation in the light of his mercy. Within the very same context of mercy, Jesus entered upon his passion and death, conscious of the great mystery of love that he would consummate on the Cross. Knowing that Jesus himself prayed this psalm makes it even more important for us as Christians, challenging us to take up the refrain in our daily lives by praying these words of praise: "for his mercy endures forever."

8. With our eyes fixed on Jesus and his merciful gaze, we experience the love of the Most Holy Trinity. The mission Jesus received from the Father was that of revealing the mystery of divine love in its fullness. "God is love" (1 Jn 4:8,16), John affirms for the first and only time in all of Holy Scripture. This love has now been made visible and tangible in Jesus' entire life. His person is nothing but love, a love given gratuitously. The relationships he forms with the people who approach him manifest something entirely unique and unrepeatable. The signs he works, especially in favour of sinners, the poor, the marginalized, the sick, and the suffering, are all meant to teach mercy. Everything in him speaks of mercy. Nothing in him is devoid of compassion.

Jesus, seeing the crowds of people who followed him, realized that they were tired and exhausted, lost and without a guide, and he felt deep compassion for them (cf. Mt 9:36). On the basis of this compassionate love he healed the sick who were presented to him (cf. Mt 14:14), and with just a few loaves of bread and fish he satisfied the enormous crowd (cf. Mt 15:37). What moved Jesus in all of these situations was nothing other than mercy, with which he read the hearts of those he encountered and responded to their deepest need. When he came upon the widow of Nain taking her son out for burial, he felt great compassion for the immense suffering of this grieving mother, and he gave back her son by raising him from the dead (cf. Lk 7:15). After freeing the demoniac in the country of the Gerasenes, Jesus entrusted him with this mission: "Go home to your friends, and tell them how much the Lord has done for you, and how he has had mercy on you" (Mk 5:19). The calling of Matthew is also presented within the context of mercy. Passing by the tax collector's booth, Jesus looked intently at Matthew. It was a look full of mercy that forgave the sins of that man, a sinner and a tax collector, whom Jesus chose – against the hesitation of the disciples – to become one of the Twelve. Saint Bede the Venerable, commenting on this Gospel passage, wrote that Jesus looked upon Matthew with merciful love and chose him: miserando atque eligendo.[7] This expression impressed me so much that I chose it for my episcopal motto.

9. In the parables devoted to mercy, Jesus reveals the nature of God as that of a Father who never gives up until he has forgiven the wrong and overcome rejection with compassion and mercy. We know these parables well, three in particular: the lost sheep, the lost coin, and the father with two sons (cf. Lk 15:1-32). In these parables, God is always presented as full of joy, especially when he pardons. In them we find the core of the Gospel and of our faith, because mercy is presented as a force that overcomes everything, filling the heart with love and bringing consolation through pardon.

From another parable, we cull an important teaching for our Christian lives. In reply to Peter's question about how many times it is necessary to forgive, Jesus says: "I do not say seven times, but seventy times seven times" (Mt 18:22). He then goes on to tell the parable of the "ruthless servant," who, called by his master to return a huge amount, begs him on his knees for mercy. His master cancels his debt. But he then meets a fellow servant who owes him a few cents and who in turn begs on his knees for mercy, but the first servant refuses his request and throws him into jail. When the master hears of the matter, he becomes infuriated and, summoning the first servant back to him, says, "Should not you have had mercy on your fellow servant, as I had mercy on you?" (Mt 18:33). Jesus concludes, "So also my heavenly Father will do to every one of you, if you do not forgive your brother from your heart" (Mt 18:35).

This parable contains a profound teaching for all of us. Jesus affirms that mercy is not only an action of the Father, it becomes a criterion for ascertaining who his true children are. In short, we are called to show mercy because mercy has first been shown to us. Pardoning offences becomes the clearest expression of merciful love, and for us Christians it is an imperative from which we cannot excuse ourselves. At times how hard it seems to forgive! And yet pardon is the instrument placed into our fragile hands to attain serenity of heart. To let go of anger, wrath, violence, and revenge are necessary conditions to living joyfully. Let us therefore heed the Apostle's exhortation: "Do not let the sun go down on your anger" (Eph 4:26). Above all, let us listen to the words of Jesus who made mercy an ideal of life and a criterion for the credibility of our faith: "Blessed are the merciful, for they shall obtain mercy" (Mt 5:7): the beatitude to which we should particularly aspire in this Holy Year.

As we can see in Sacred Scripture, mercy is a key word that indicates God's action towards us. He does not limit himself merely to affirming his love, but makes it visible and tangible. Love, after all, can never be just an abstraction. By its very nature, it indicates something concrete: intentions, attitudes, and behaviours that are shown in daily living. The mercy of God is his loving concern for each one of us. He feels responsible; that is, he desires our wellbeing and he wants to see us happy, full of joy, and peaceful. This is the path which the merciful love of Christians must also travel. As the Father loves, so do his children. Just as he is merciful, so we are called to be merciful to each other.

10. Mercy is the very foundation of the Church's life. All of her pastoral activity should be caught up in the tenderness she makes present to believers; nothing in her preaching and in her witness to the world can be lacking in mercy. The Church's very credibility is seen in how she shows merciful and compassionate love. The Church "has an endless desire to show mercy".[8] Perhaps we have long since forgotten how to show and live the way of mercy. The temptation, on the one hand, to focus exclusively on justice made us forget that this is only the first, albeit necessary and indispensable step. But the Church needs to go beyond and strive for a higher and more important goal. On the other hand, sad to say, we must admit that the practice of mercy is waning in the wider culture. In some cases the word seems to have dropped out of use. However, without a witness to mercy, life becomes fruitless and sterile, as if sequestered in a barren desert. The time has come for the Church to take up the joyful call to mercy once more. It is time to return to the basics and to bear the weaknesses and struggles of our brothers and sisters. Mercy is the force that reawakens us to new life and instils in us the courage to look to the future with hope.

11. Let us not forget the great teaching offered by Saint John Paul II in his second Encyclical, Dives in Misericordia, which at the time came unexpectedly, its theme catching many by surprise. There are two passages in particular to which I would like to draw attention. First, Saint John Paul II highlighted the fact that we had forgotten the theme of mercy in today's cultural milieu: "The present-day mentality,

more perhaps than that of people in the past, seems opposed to a God of mercy, and in fact tends to exclude from life and to remove from the human heart the very idea of mercy. The word and the concept of 'mercy' seem to cause uneasiness in man, who, thanks to the enormous development of science and technology, never before known in history, has become the master of the earth and has subdued and dominated it (cf. Gen 1:28). This dominion over the earth, sometimes understood in a one-sided and superficial way, seems to have no room for mercy... And this is why, in the situation of the Church and the world today, many individuals and groups guided by a lively sense of faith are turning, I would say almost spontaneously, to the mercy of God".[9]

Furthermore, Saint John Paul II pushed for a more urgent proclamation and witness to mercy in the contemporary world: "It is dictated by love for man, for all that is human and which, according to the intuitions of many of our contemporaries, is threatened by an immense danger. The mystery of Christ... obliges me to proclaim mercy as God's merciful love, revealed in that same mystery of Christ. It likewise obliges me to have recourse to that mercy and to beg for it at this difficult, critical phase of the history of the Church and of the world".[10] This teaching is more pertinent than ever and deserves to be taken up once again in this Holy Year. Let us listen to his words once more: "The Church lives an authentic life when she professes and proclaims mercy – the most stupendous attribute of the Creator and of the Redeemer – and when she brings people close to the sources of the Saviour's mercy, of which she is the trustee and dispenser".[11]

12. The Church is commissioned to announce the mercy of God, the beating heart of the Gospel, which in its own way must penetrate the heart and mind of every person. The Spouse of Christ must pattern her behaviour after the Son of

God who went out to everyone without exception. In the present day, as the Church is charged with the task of the new evangelization, the theme of mercy needs to be proposed again and again with new enthusiasm and renewed pastoral action. It is absolutely essential for the Church and for the credibility of her message that she herself live and testify to mercy. Her language and her gestures must transmit mercy, so as to touch the hearts of all people and inspire them once more to find the road that leads to the Father.

The Church's first truth is the love of Christ. The Church makes herself a servant of this love and mediates it to all people: a love that forgives and expresses itself in the gift of oneself. Consequently, wherever the Church is present, the mercy of the Father must be evident. In our parishes, communities, associations and movements, in a word, wherever there are Christians, everyone should find an oasis of mercy.

13. We want to live this Jubilee Year in light of the Lord's words: Merciful like the Father. The Evangelist reminds us of the teaching of Jesus who says, "Be merciful just as your Father is merciful" (Lk 6:36). It is a programme of life as demanding as it is rich with joy and peace. Jesus's command is directed to anyone willing to listen to his voice (cf. Lk 6:27). In order to be capable of mercy, therefore, we must first of all dispose ourselves to listen to the Word of God. This means rediscovering the value of silence in order to meditate on the Word that comes to us. In this way, it will be possible to contemplate God's mercy and adopt it as our lifestyle.

14. The practice of pilgrimage has a special place in the Holy Year, because it represents the journey each of us makes in this life. Life itself is a pilgrimage, and the human being is a viator, a pilgrim travelling along the road, making his way to the desired destination. Similarly, to reach the

Holy Door in Rome or in any other place in the world, everyone, each according to his or her ability, will have to make a pilgrimage. This will be a sign that mercy is also a goal to reach and requires dedication and sacrifice. May pilgrimage be an impetus to conversion: by crossing the threshold of the Holy Door, we will find the strength to embrace God's mercy and dedicate ourselves to being merciful with others as the Father has been with us.

The Lord Jesus shows us the steps of the pilgrimage to attain our goal: "Judge not, and you will not be judged; condemn not, and you will not be condemned; forgive, and you will be forgiven; give, and it will be given to you; good measure, pressed down, shaken together, running over, will be put into your lap. For the measure you give will be the measure you get back" (Lk 6:37-38). The Lord asks us above all not to judge and not to condemn. If anyone wishes to avoid God's judgement, he should not make himself the judge of his brother or sister. Human beings, whenever they judge, look no farther than the surface, whereas the Father looks into the very depths of the soul. How much harm words do when they are motivated by feelings of jealousy and envy! To speak ill of others puts them in a bad light, undermines their reputation and leaves them prey to the whims of gossip. To refrain from judgement and condemnation means, in a positive sense, to know how to accept the good in every person and to spare him any suffering that might be caused by our partial judgment, our presumption to know everything about him. But this is still not sufficient to express mercy. Jesus asks us also to forgive and to give. To be instruments of mercy because it was we who first received mercy from God. To be generous with others, knowing that God showers his goodness upon us with immense generosity.

Merciful like the Father, therefore, is the "motto" of this Holy Year. In mercy, we find proof of how God loves us. He gives his entire self, always, freely, asking nothing in return. He comes to our aid whenever we call upon him. What a beautiful thing that the Church begins her daily prayer with the words, "O God, come to my assistance. O Lord, make haste to help me" (Ps 70:2)! The assistance we ask for is already the first step of God's mercy toward us. He comes to assist us in our weakness. And his help consists in helping us accept his presence and closeness to us. Day after day, touched by his compassion, we also can become compassionate towards others.

15. In this Holy Year, we look forward to the experience of opening our hearts to those living on the outermost fringes of society: fringes which modern society itself creates. How many uncertain and painful situations there are in the world today! How many are the wounds borne by the flesh of those who have no voice because their cry is muffled and drowned out by the indifference of the rich! During this Jubilee, the Church will be called even more to heal these wounds, to assuage them with the oil of consolation, to bind them with mercy and cure them with solidarity and vigilant care. Let us not fall into humiliating indifference or a monotonous routine that prevents us from discovering what is new! Let us ward off destructive cynicism! Let us open our eyes and see the misery of the world, the wounds of our brothers and sisters who are denied their dignity, and let us recognize that we are compelled to heed their cry for help! May we reach out to them and support them so they can feel the warmth of our presence, our friendship, and our fraternity! May their cry become our own, and together may we break down the barriers of indifference that too often reign supreme and mask our hypocrisy and egoism!

It is my burning desire that, during this Jubilee, the Christian people may reflect on the corporal and spiritual works of mercy. It will be a way to reawaken our conscience, too often grown dull in the face of poverty. And let us enter more deeply into the heart of the Gospel where the poor have a special experience of God's mercy. Jesus introduces us to these works of mercy in his preaching so that we can know whether or not we are living as his disciples. Let us rediscover these corporal works of mercy: to feed the hungry, give drink to the thirsty, clothe the naked, welcome the stranger, heal the sick, visit the imprisoned, and bury the dead. And let us not forget the spiritual works of mercy: to counsel the doubtful, instruct the ignorant, admonish sinners, comfort the afflicted, forgive offences, bear patiently those who do us ill, and pray for the living and the dead.

We cannot escape the Lord's words to us, and they will serve as the criteria upon which we will be judged: whether we have fed the hungry and given drink to the thirsty, welcomed the stranger and clothed the naked, or spent time with the sick and those in prison (cf. Mt 25:31-45). Moreover, we will be asked if we have helped others to escape the doubt that causes them to fall into despair and which is often a source of loneliness; if we have helped to overcome the ignorance in which millions of people live, especially children deprived of the necessary means to free them from the bonds of poverty; if we have been close to the lonely and afflicted; if we have forgiven those who have offended us and have rejected all forms of anger and hate that lead to violence; if we have had the kind of patience God shows, who is so patient with us; and if we have commended our brothers and sisters to the Lord in prayer. In each of these "little ones," Christ himself is present. His flesh becomes visible in the flesh of the tortured, the crushed, the scourged, the malnourished, and the exiled... to be acknowledged, touched, and cared for by us. Let us not forget the words of Saint John of the Cross: "as we prepare to leave this life, we will be judged on the basis of love".[12]

16. In the Gospel of Luke, we find another important element that will help us live the Jubilee with faith. Luke writes that Jesus, on the Sabbath, went back to Nazareth and, as was his custom, entered the synagogue. They called upon him to read the Scripture and to comment on it. The passage was from the Book of Isaiah where it is written: "The Spirit of the Lord God is upon me, because the Lord has anointed me to bring good tidings to the afflicted; he has sent me to bind up the brokenhearted, to proclaim liberty to the captives, and freedom to those in captivity; to proclaim the year of the Lord's favour" (Is 61:1-2). A "year of the Lord's favour" or "mercy": this is what the Lord proclaimed and this is what we wish to live now. This Holy Year will bring to the fore the richness of Jesus' mission echoed in the words of the prophet: to bring a word and gesture of consolation to the poor, to proclaim liberty to those bound by new forms of slavery in modern society, to restore sight to those who can see no more because they are caught up in themselves, to restore dignity to all those from whom it has been robbed. The preaching of Jesus is made visible once more in the response of faith which Christians are called to offer by their witness. May the words of the Apostle accompany us: he who does acts of mercy, let him do them with cheerfulness (cf. Rom 12:8).

17. The season of Lent during this Jubilee Year should also be lived more intensely as a privileged moment to celebrate and experience God's mercy. How many pages of Sacred Scripture are appropriate for meditation during the weeks of Lent to help us rediscover the merciful face of the Father! We can repeat the words of the prophet Micah and make them our own: You, O Lord, are a God who takes away

iniquity and pardons sin, who does not hold your anger forever, but are pleased to show mercy. You, Lord, will return to us and have pity on your people. You will trample down our sins and toss them into the depths of the sea (cf. 7:18-19).

The pages of the prophet Isaiah can also be meditated upon concretely during this season of prayer, fasting, and works of charity: "Is not this the fast that I choose: to loosen the bonds of wickedness, to undo the thongs of the yoke, to let the oppressed go free, and to break every yoke? Is it not to share your bread with the hungry, and bring the homeless poor into your house; when you see the naked, to cover him, and not to hide yourself from your own flesh? Then shall your light break forth like the dawn, and your healing shall spring up speedily; your righteousness shall go before you, the glory of the Lord shall be your rear guard. Then you shall call, and the Lord will answer; you shall cry, and he will say, here I am. If you take away from the midst of you the yoke, the pointing of the finger, and speaking wickedness, if you pour yourself out for the hungry and satisfy the desire of the afflicted, then shall your light rise in the darkness and your gloom be as the noonday. And the Lord will guide you continually, and satisfy your desire with good things, and make your bones strong; and you shall be like a watered garden, like a spring of water, whose waters fail not" (58:6-11).

The initiative of "24 Hours for the Lord," to be celebrated on the Friday and Saturday preceding the Fourth Week of Lent, should be implemented in every diocese. So many people, including young people, are returning to the Sacrament of Reconciliation; through this experience they are rediscovering a path back to the Lord, living a moment of intense prayer and finding meaning in their lives. Let us place the Sacrament of Reconciliation at the centre once more in such a way that it will enable people to touch the grandeur of God's mercy with their own hands. For every penitent, it will be a source of true interior peace.

I will never tire of insisting that confessors be authentic signs of the Father's mercy. We do not become good confessors automatically. We become good confessors when, above all, we allow ourselves to be penitents in search of his mercy. Let us never forget that to be confessors means to participate in the very mission of Jesus to be a concrete sign of the constancy of divine love that pardons and saves. We priests have received the gift of the Holy Spirit for the forgiveness of sins, and we are responsible for this. None of us wields power over this Sacrament; rather, we are faithful servants of God's mercy through it. Every confessor must accept the faithful as the father in the parable of the prodigal son: a father who runs out to meet his son despite the fact that he has squandered away his inheritance. Confessors are called to embrace the repentant son who comes back home and to express the joy of having him back again. Let us never tire of also going out to the other son who stands outside, incapable of rejoicing, in order to explain to him that his judgement is severe and unjust and meaningless in light of the father's boundless mercy. May confessors not ask useless questions, but like the father in the parable, interrupt the speech prepared ahead of time by the prodigal son, so that confessors will learn to accept the plea for help and mercy pouring from the heart of every penitent. In short, confessors are called to be a sign of the primacy of mercy always, everywhere, and in every situation, no matter what.

18. During Lent of this Holy Year, I intend to send out Missionaries of Mercy. They will be a sign of the Church's maternal solicitude for the People of God, enabling them to enter the profound richness of this mystery so fundamental to the faith. There will be priests to whom I will grant the

authority to pardon even those sins reserved to the Holy See, so that the breadth of their mandate as confessors will be even clearer. They will be, above all, living signs of the Father's readiness to welcome those in search of his pardon. They will be missionaries of mercy because they will be facilitators of a truly human encounter, a source of liberation, rich with responsibility for overcoming obstacles and taking up the new life of Baptism again. They will be led in their mission by the words of the Apostle: "For God has consigned all men to disobedience, that he may have mercy upon all" (Rom 11:32). Everyone, in fact, without exception, is called to embrace the call to mercy. May these Missionaries live this call with the assurance that they can fix their eyes on Jesus, "the merciful and faithful high priest in the service of God" (Heb 2:17).

I ask my brother Bishops to invite and welcome these Missionaries so that they can be, above all, persuasive preachers of mercy. May individual dioceses organize "missions to the people" in such a way that these Missionaries may be heralds of joy and forgiveness. Bishops are asked to celebrate the Sacrament of Reconciliation with their people so that the time of grace made possible by the Jubilee year makes it possible for many of God's sons and daughters to take up once again the journey to the Father's house. May pastors, especially during the liturgical season of Lent, be diligent in calling back the faithful "to the throne of grace, that we may receive mercy and find grace" (Heb 4:16).

19. May the message of mercy reach everyone, and may no one be indifferent to the call to experience mercy. I direct this invitation to conversion even more fervently to those whose behaviour distances them from the grace of God. I particularly have in mind men and women belonging to criminal organizations of any kind. For their own good, I beg them to change their lives. I ask them this in the name of the

Son of God who, though rejecting sin, never rejected the sinner. Do not fall into the terrible trap of thinking that life depends on money and that, in comparison with money, anything else is devoid of value or dignity. This is nothing but an illusion! We cannot take money with us into the life beyond. Money does not bring us happiness. Violence inflicted for the sake of amassing riches soaked in blood makes one neither powerful nor immortal. Everyone, sooner or later, will be subject to God's judgment, from which no one can escape.

The same invitation is extended to those who either perpetrate or participate in corruption. This festering wound is a grave sin that cries out to heaven for vengeance, because it threatens the very foundations of personal and social life. Corruption prevents us from looking to the future with hope, because its tyrannical greed shatters the plans of the weak and tramples upon the poorest of the poor. It is an evil that embeds itself into the actions of everyday life and spreads, causing great public scandal. Corruption is a sinful hardening of the heart that replaces God with the illusion that money is a form of power. It is a work of darkness, fed by suspicion and intrigue. Corruptio optimi pessima, saint Gregory the Great said with good reason, affirming that no one can think himself immune from this temptation. If we want to drive it out from personal and social life, we need prudence, vigilance, loyalty, transparency, together with the courage to denounce any wrongdoing. If it is not combated openly, sooner or later everyone will become an accomplice to it, and it will end up destroying our very existence.

This is the opportune moment to change our lives! This is the time to allow our hearts to be touched! When faced with evil deeds, even in the face of serious crimes, it is the time to listen to the cry of innocent people who are deprived of their property, their dignity, their feelings, and even their very lives. To stick to the way of evil will only leave one deluded and sad. True life is something entirely different. God never tires of reaching out to us. He is always ready to listen, as I am too, along with my brother bishops and priests. All one needs to do is to accept the invitation to conversion and submit oneself to justice during this special time of mercy offered by the Church.

20. It would not be out of place at this point to recall the relationship between justice and mercy. These are not two contradictory realities, but two dimensions of a single reality that unfolds progressively until it culminates in the fullness of love. Justice is a fundamental concept for civil society, which is meant to be governed by the rule of law. Justice is also understood as that which is rightly due to each individual. In the Bible, there are many references to divine justice and to God as "judge". In these passages, justice is understood as the full observance of the Law and the behaviour of every good Israelite in conformity with God's commandments. Such a vision, however, has not infrequently led to legalism by distorting the original meaning of justice and obscuring its profound value. To overcome this legalistic perspective, we need to recall that in Sacred Scripture, justice is conceived essentially as the faithful abandonment of oneself to God's will.

For his part, Jesus speaks several times of the importance of faith over and above the observance of the law. It is in this sense that we must understand his words when, reclining at table with Matthew and other tax collectors and sinners, he says to the Pharisees raising objections to him, "Go and learn the meaning of 'I desire mercy not sacrifice'. I have come not to call the righteous, but sinners" (Mt 9:13). Faced with a vision of justice as the mere observance of the law that judges people simply by dividing them into two groups – the just and sinners – Jesus is bent on revealing the great gift of mercy that searches out sinners and offers them pardon and salvation. One can see why, on the basis of such a liberating vision of mercy as a source of new life, Jesus was rejected by the Pharisees and the other teachers of the law. In an attempt to remain faithful to the law, they merely placed burdens on the shoulders of others and undermined the Father's mercy. The appeal to a faithful observance of the law must not prevent attention from being given to matters that touch upon the dignity of the person.

The appeal Jesus makes to the text from the book of the prophet Hosea – "I desire love and not sacrifice" (6:6) – is important in this regard. Jesus affirms that, from that time onward, the rule of life for his disciples must place mercy at the centre, as Jesus himself demonstrated by sharing meals with sinners. Mercy, once again, is revealed as a fundamental aspect of Jesus' mission. This is truly challenging to his hearers, who would draw the line at a formal respect for the law. Jesus, on the other hand, goes beyond the law; the company he keeps with those the law considers sinners makes us realize the depth of his mercy.

The Apostle Paul makes a similar journey. Prior to meeting Jesus on the road to Damascus, he dedicated his life to pursuing the justice of the law with zeal (cf. Phil 3:6). His conversion to Christ led him to turn that vision upside down, to the point that he would write to the Galatians: "We have believed in Christ Jesus, in order to be justified by faith in Christ, and not by works of the law, because by works of the law shall no one be justified" (2:16).

Paul's understanding of justice changes radically. He now places faith first, not justice. Salvation comes not through the observance of the law, but through faith in Jesus Christ, who in his death and resurrection brings salvation together with a mercy that justifies. God's justice now becomes the liberating force for those oppressed by slavery to sin and its consequences. God's justice is his mercy (cf. Ps 51:11-16).

21. Mercy is not opposed to justice but rather expresses God's way of reaching out to the sinner, offering him a new chance to look at himself, convert, and believe. The experience of the prophet Hosea can help us see the way in which mercy surpasses justice. The era in which the prophet lived was one of the most dramatic in the history of the Jewish people. The kingdom was tottering on the edge of destruction; the people had not remained faithful to the covenant; they had wandered from God and lost the faith of their forefathers. According to human logic, it seems reasonable for God to think of rejecting an unfaithful people; they had not observed their pact with God and therefore deserved just punishment: in other words, exile. The prophet's words attest to this: "They shall not return to the land of Egypt, and Assyria shall be their king, because they have refused to return to me" (Hos 11:5). And yet, after this invocation of justice, the prophet radically changes his speech and reveals the true face of God: "How can I give you up, O Ephraim! How can I hand you over, O Israel! How can I make you like Admah! How can I treat you like Zeboiim! My heart recoils within me, my compassion grows warm and tender. I will not execute my fierce anger, I will not again destroy Ephraim; for I am God and not man, the Holy One in your midst, and I will not come to destroy" (11:8-9). Saint Augustine, almost as if he were commenting on these words of the prophet, says: "It is easier for God to hold back anger than mercy".[13] And so it is. God's anger lasts but a moment, his mercy forever.

If God limited himself to only justice, he would cease to be God, and would instead be like human beings who ask merely that the law be respected. But mere justice is not enough. Experience shows that an appeal to justice alone will result in its destruction. This is why God goes beyond justice with his mercy and forgiveness. Yet this does not mean that justice should be devalued or rendered superfluous. On the contrary: anyone who makes a mistake must pay the price. However, this is just the beginning of conversion, not its end, because one begins to feel the tenderness and mercy of God. God does not deny justice. He rather envelopes it and surpasses it with an even greater event in which we experience love as the foundation of true justice. We must pay close attention to what Saint Paul says if we want to avoid making the same mistake for which he reproaches the Jews of his time: "For, being ignorant of the righteousness that comes from God, and seeking to establish their own, they did not submit to God's righteousness. For Christ is the end of the law, that every one who has faith may be justified" (Rom 10:3-4). God's justice is his mercy given to everyone as a grace that flows from the death and resurrection of Jesus Christ. Thus the Cross of Christ is God's judgement on all of us and on the whole world, because through it he offers us the certitude of love and new life.

22. A Jubilee also entails the granting of indulgences. This practice will acquire an even more important meaning in the Holy Year of Mercy. God's forgiveness knows no bounds. In the death and resurrection of Jesus Christ, God makes even more evident his love and its power to destroy all human sin. Reconciliation with God is made possible through the paschal mystery and the mediation of the Church. Thus God is always ready to forgive, and he never tires of forgiving in ways that are continually new and surprising. Nevertheless, all of us know well the experience of sin. We know that we are called to perfection (cf. Mt 5:48), yet we feel the heavy burden of sin. Though we feel the transforming power of grace, we also feel the effects of sin typical of our fallen state. Despite being forgiven, the

conflicting consequences of our sins remain. In the Sacrament of Reconciliation, God forgives our sins, which he truly blots out; and yet sin leaves a negative effect on the way we think and act. But the mercy of God is stronger even than this. It becomes indulgence on the part of the Father who, through the Bride of Christ, his Church, reaches the pardoned sinner and frees him from every residue left by the consequences of sin, enabling him to act with charity, to grow in love rather than to fall back into sin.

The Church lives within the communion of the saints. In the Eucharist, this communion, which is a gift from God, becomes a spiritual union binding us to the saints and blessed ones whose number is beyond counting (cf. Rev 7:4). Their holiness comes to the aid of our weakness in a way that enables the Church, with her maternal prayers and her way of life, to fortify the weakness of some with the strength of others. Hence, to live the indulgence of the Holy Year means to approach the Father's mercy with the certainty that his forgiveness extends to the entire life of the believer. To gain an indulgence is to experience the holiness of the Church, who bestows upon all the fruits of Christ's redemption, so that God's love and forgiveness may extend everywhere. Let us live this Jubilee intensely, begging the Father to forgive our sins and to bathe us in his merciful "indulgence."

23. There is an aspect of mercy that goes beyond the confines of the Church. It relates us to Judaism and Islam, both of which consider mercy to be one of God's most important attributes. Israel was the first to receive this revelation which continues in history as the source of an inexhaustible richness meant to be shared with all mankind. As we have seen, the pages of the Old Testament are steeped in mercy, because they narrate the works that the Lord performed in favour of his people at the most trying moments of their history. Among the privileged names that

Islam attributes to the Creator are "Merciful and Kind". This invocation is often on the lips of faithful Muslims who feel themselves accompanied and sustained by mercy in their daily weakness. They too believe that no one can place a limit on divine mercy because its doors are always open.

I trust that this Jubilee year celebrating the mercy of God will foster an encounter with these religions and with other noble religious traditions; may it open us to even more fervent dialogue so that we might know and understand one another better; may it eliminate every form of closed-mindedness and disrespect, and drive out every form of violence and discrimination.

24. My thoughts now turn to the Mother of Mercy. May the sweetness of her countenance watch over us in this Holy Year, so that all of us may rediscover the joy of God's tenderness. No one has penetrated the profound mystery of the incarnation like Mary. Her entire life was patterned after the presence of mercy made flesh. The Mother of the Crucified and Risen One has entered the sanctuary of divine mercy because she participated intimately in the mystery of His love.

Chosen to be the Mother of the Son of God, Mary, from the outset, was prepared by the love of God to be the Ark of the Covenant between God and man. She treasured divine mercy in her heart in perfect harmony with her Son Jesus. Her hymn of praise, sung at the threshold of the home of Elizabeth, was dedicated to the mercy of God which extends from "generation to generation" (Lk 1:50). We too were included in those prophetic words of the Virgin Mary. This will be a source of comfort and strength to us as we cross the threshold of the Holy Year to experience the fruits of divine mercy.

At the foot of the Cross, Mary, together with John, the disciple of love, witnessed the words of forgiveness spoken by Jesus. This supreme expression of mercy towards those who crucified him show us the point to which the mercy of God can reach. Mary attests that the mercy of the Son of God knows no bounds and extends to everyone, without exception. Let us address her in the words of the Salve Regina, a prayer ever ancient and ever new, so that she may never tire of turning her merciful eyes upon us, and make us worthy to contemplate the face of mercy, her Son Jesus.

Our prayer also extends to the saints and blessed ones who made divine mercy their mission in life. I think especially of the great apostle of mercy, Saint Faustina Kowalska. May she, who was called to enter the depths of divine mercy, intercede for us and obtain for us the grace of living and walking always according to the mercy of God and with an unwavering trust in his love.

25. I present, therefore, this Extraordinary Jubilee Year dedicated to living out in our daily lives the mercy which the Father constantly extends to all of us. In this Jubilee Year, let us allow God to surprise us. He never tires of casting open the doors of his heart and of repeating that he loves us and wants to share his love with us. The Church feels the urgent need to proclaim God's mercy. Her life is authentic and credible only when she becomes a convincing herald of mercy. She knows that her primary task, especially at a moment full of great hopes and signs of contradiction, is to introduce everyone to the great mystery of God's mercy by contemplating the face of Christ. The Church is called above all to be a credible witness to mercy, professing it and living it as the core of the revelation of Jesus Christ. From the heart of the Trinity, from the depths of the mystery of God, the great river of mercy wells up and overflows unceasingly. It is a spring that will never run dry, no matter how many people draw from it. Every time someone is in need, he or she can approach it, because the mercy of God never ends. The

profundity of the mystery surrounding it is as inexhaustible as the richness which springs up from it.

In this Jubilee Year, may the Church echo the word of God that resounds strong and clear as a message and a sign of pardon, strength, aid, and love. May she never tire of extending mercy, and be ever patient in offering compassion and comfort. May the Church become the voice of every man and woman, and repeat confidently without end: "Be mindful of your mercy, O Lord, and your steadfast love, for they have been from of old" (Ps 25:6).

Given in Rome, at Saint Peter's, on 11 April, the Vigil of the Second Sunday of Easter, or the Sunday of Divine Mercy, in the year of our Lord 2015, the third of my Pontificate.

FRANCISCUS

[1] Cf. Second Vatican Ecumenical Council, Dogmatic Constitution on Divine Revelation Dei Verbum, 4.

[2] Opening Address of the Second Vatican Ecumenical Council, Gaudet Mater Ecclesia, 11 October 1962, 2-3.

[3] Speech at the Final Public Session of the Second Vatican Ecumenical Council, 7 December 1965.

[4] Cf. Second Vatican Ecumenical Council, Dogmatic Constitution on the Church Lumen Gentium, 16: Pastoral Constitution on the Church in the Modern World Gaudium et Spes, 15.

[5] Saint Thomas Aquinas, Summa Theologiae, II-II, q. 30. a. 4.

[6] XXVI Sunday in Ordinary Time. This Collect already appears in the eighth century among the euchological texts of the Gelasian Sacramentary (1198).

[7] Cf. Homily 22: CCL, 122, 149-151.

[8] Apostolic Exhortation Evangelii Gaudium, 24.

[9] No. 2.

[10] Saint John Paul II, Encyclical Letter Dives in Misericordia, 15.

[11] Ibid., 13.

[12] Words of Light and Love, 57.

[13] Homilies on the Psalms, 76, 11.

GLOSSARY

Syllable: A vocal sound or set of sounds uttered with a single effort of articulation and forming a word or an element of a word; each of the elements of spoken language comprising a sound of greater sonority (vowel or vowel-equivalent) with or without one or more sounds of less sonority (consonants or consonant-equivalents); also, a character or set of characters forming a corresponding element of written language.

Foot: is a measuring unit in poetry, which is made up of stressed and unstressed syllables. The stressed syllable is generally indicated by a vertical line (|), whereas the unstressed syllable is represented by a cross (X).

Meter: is a stressed and unstressed syllabic pattern in a verse, or within the lines of a poem. Stressed syllables tend to be longer, and unstressed shorter. In simple language, meter is a poetic device that serves as a linguistic sound pattern for the verses, as it gives poetry a rhythmical and melodious sound.

Iambic Pentameter: Iambic pentameter refers to the pattern or rhythm of a line of poetry or verse and has to do with the number of syllables in the line and the emphasis placed on those syllables. William Shakespeare's works are often used as great examples of iambic pentameter.

Pyrrhic: a metrical foot consisting of two short or unaccented syllables. It is also a metrical foot consisting of two short or unaccented syllables.

Anaphora: repetition of a word or expression at the beginning of successive phrases, clauses, sentences, or verses especially for rhetorical or poetic effect.

Masculine Ending: refers to a line ending in a stressed syllable.

Feminine Ending: describes a line ending in a stressless syllable.

Stressed Syllabus: is the syllable that a native British English speaker would bring attention to by way of changing the pitch of their voice.

Spondee: is a beat in a poetic line that consists of two accented syllables (stressed/stressed) or DUM-DUM stress pattern. Spondee is a poetic device that is not as common as other metrical feet, like Iamb and trochee.

Scansion: means looking at the words, dividing them into syllables, marking the longs and shorts, marking the feet.

BIBLIOGRAPHY

Cantalamessa, OFM. Cap. Raniero, *Beautitudes: Eight Steps to Happiness* (Transl.) Marsha Daigle-Williamson. Cincinnati, Ohio: Servant, 2009.

Chapman, Geoffrey, Catechism of the Catholic Church (Popular and Definitive Edition). India: Thompson Press. 2000.

Dolan, Cardinal Timothy. *Priests for the Third Millennium.* Huntington. Our Sunday Visitor Publishing Division. 2000.

Flannery, Austin (Gen. Ed.), Vatican II document: The Conciliar and Post Conciliar Documents, St. Paul's, Mumbai, 2001.

Fisch, Harold. "The Song of Moses: Pastoral in Reverse." In *Poetry with a Purpose: Biblical Poetics and Interpretation*, page 55. Bloomington, Indiana: Indiana University Press, 1990. ISBN 0-253-34557-X.

John Paul II, *Discourse. Partecipazione dei fedeli llaici al ministero presbyterale,* April 22, 1994, English trans, in *Observatore Romanon* May 1, 1994 and Origins 24 (June 4, 1994). Flannery, Austin, O.P., Vatican Council II: More Post Conciliar Documents (Evangelii Nuntiandi 14)

Kloppenburg, O.F.M., Bonaventure. *The Ecclesiology of Vatican II*, Franciscan Herald Press, Chicago, 1974.

Lahaye, Tim. *Spirit-Controlled Temperament.* Tyndale House Publishers, Inc. Ilinois. 1992.

Pantazakos, Michael. "Shylock's Forced Conversion." *Cardozo Studies in Law and Literature*, Vol. 5, No.2. Taylor & Francis Ltd. 1993, pp. 338-356.

Pope Francis. *The Name of God is Mercy* (Transl) Oonagh Stransky. New York: Random House, 2016.

Pope Francis. *Men of Mercy: Pope Francis Speaks to Priests.* Edited by Giuseppe Merola. Beacon Publishing. 2016.

Rev. Bro. Agyemang (SVD). "Before The Council" *The Standard* (Vol. 73, No. 37), 2010.

ABOUT THE AUTHOR

Rev. Fr. Aaron Agbeshie Agorsor is a priest of the Catholic Archdiocese of Accra, Ghana, West Africa. He is currently a Ph.D. student of English Literature at the Arizona State University.

As a Graduate Assistant, he teaches First Year Writing or composition and assists at ASU affiliated All Saints Catholic Newman Centre where he ministers to students from diverse backgrounds.

Fr. Aaron is passionate about his ministry as a priest. His experience of God's tremendous mercy overwhelms him and he wishes to let the whole world know that God's mercy endures forever. He is also the author of *Mary's Magnificat: A Perfect Model of Faith Expression.*

Made in USA - Kendallville, IN
1079089_9781952464041
04.14.2020 0807